T0277581

BRAZIL
1970

BRAZIL
1970

HOW THE
GREATEST TEAM OF ALL TIME
WON THE WORLD CUP

SAM KUNTI

First published by Pitch Publishing, 2022

Pitch Publishing
9 Donnington Park,
85 Birdham Road,
Chichester,
West Sussex,
PO20 7AJ
www.pitchpublishing.co.uk
info@pitchpublishing.co.uk

A CIP catalogue record is available for this book
from the British Library.

ISBN 978 1 80150 360 0

Typesetting and origination by Pitch Publishing

Printed and bound in Great Britain by TJ Books, Padstow

Contents

Foreword

I FEEL privileged because, in 1970, I managed to help Brazil win the Jules Rimet Trophy. The team that won the World Cup three times would take her home for good. Brazil won and I had a helping hand.

I want to praise the coaching staff of Mário Lobo Zagallo, Admildo Chirol, [Raul] Carlesso and [Kleber] Camerino. They were important people in the strategy we put together to play in this World Cup. And thanks to my team-mates, who were of an outstanding technical level.

We prepared for every aspect of the competition, especially for playing at altitude. There was a specific oxygen preparation that contributed to our success and reaching the final at the Azteca Stadium. We already had a high level of harmony in the squad ahead of the competition after a beautiful three-month preparation. Those training camps provided us with everything: great fitness and tactical understanding. And most importantly, forming the team and the collective, integrating each individual.

We went to Guanajuato, a city at very high altitude, and that improved our natural fitness and increased our red blood cells. By doing this, we also grew our stamina. I remember that in the tournament in the first half of the matches our opponents matched us physically, but in the second half Brazil completely overwhelmed them.

Without a doubt, Mexico 1970 was my peak. You don't know how hard it was for me to take on the responsibility of replacing my idol – just imagine, replacing Garrincha. But I'm sure everyone in Brazil and across the world recognises that, after Garrincha, the greatest right-winger ever to emerge in world football was Jairzinho.

Before the opening match against Czechoslovakia, we got together. It was just us, the players. The backroom staff didn't participate. That's when we decided that it was Brazil that had to win, and not Jairzinho, not Pelé, not Rivellino, not Tostão, not Gérson, and not Félix. We'd win together because we wanted to achieve two very important things: firstly, to win the title and, with it, to claim the Jules Rimet Trophy forever.

From the first match on, we received the support of the Mexican fans. That gave us a peace of mind. They lined the sidewalks. When we started to go into the stadium, they stopped in front of our bus and the escorts that we had, wishing us all good luck. That was unforgettable, especially for me, that act of motivation, this act of encouragement from the Mexicans.

The match against England came with great expectations and a lot of coverage from the press. In the days leading up to the match, it was written that that the world was going to witness the real final. And it was, in fact, a game of great quality – emotionally, physically, tactically and creatively. For me, two players were at the heart of the big spectacle: Banks for England and Félix for Brazil. I've never seen two goalkeepers save as much as Banks and Félix did.

It was my goal that won us the World Cup. I'm sure most of my team-mates, or even all, said that was the decisive one. Pelé was surrounded by three or four English defenders and the ball came straight to him. He pretended to shoot but controlled the ball. I was outside him, about five metres away. He passed it and I closed in on Banks. I pretended to shoot first, Banks went down and I hit the ball diagonally, and it flew in fantastically.

You have no idea what it's like to score a goal, especially in a World Cup. To this day, I'm still the only player who has scored in every match in a World Cup. When we scored the third against Italy, practically all of us thought the same thing: 'There's no chance they'll get a draw or even beat us.' The third goal was crucial for our calmness and increased the unease of the opponents.

It's hard to describe what it means to be a world champion. It was sensational, exciting and thrilling. Brazilians were experiencing a time of military dictatorship. For our matches … Brazil stopped. People stopped working, stopped studying, stopped everything to watch us play, and it was the biggest pandemonium in the lives of Brazilians to this day, seeing the 1970 team show the world why it was the best.

Of course, every day when I wake up I remember my accomplishment and my team-mates from 1970, and when I go to sleep I thank God for having been one of the greatest players in the world. The team of 1970 was one of the best ever. I would again like to say what a happy guy I am, because I had the opportunity to make Brazil, once again, be recognised in world football.

The *tricampeonato* was unforgettable.

Jair Ventura Filho 'Jairzinho', Rio de Janeiro,
March 2022

Introduction

I BELONG to the generation that in the late 1990s fell for Nike's brilliant sales pitch: 'Brazil have a dream team again! They are ready to win the 1998 World Cup!' Spearheaded by the buck-toothed Ronaldo, a select of Brazilian stars dribbled their way through Rio de Janeiro's airport to the infectious tunes of Jorge Ben's 'Mas Que Nada'. It's an advert that most remember. Its end possibly less so – Ronaldo fails to score, just as he did in the 1998 World Cup Final. Once in France, the Seleção didn't quite deliver on the sportswear giant's promise. They showed glimpses of brilliance against the Netherlands in the last four but, in general, Brazil were disappointing, at least in the eyes of a ten-year-old.

Nike had oversold the dream team but the myth endured: the Brazilians supposedly played divine football. Over the next two decades, there was little evidence of their mythical status as I travelled to watch and cover Brazil from Miami to Kazan – the graveyard of the great, where Brazil fell flat against Belgium, my home country. Sometimes it was hard to believe in the beautiful game.

I watched Carlos Alberto Torres's wonder strike against Italy for the first time on video when I was a kid. That goal wasn't a sales pitch. It was poetry. Simply magical. I was transfixed.

In 2008 I met Carlos Alberto for the first time. We shared breakfast at Schiphol Airport's Ibis and drove to a small village in the Dutch polder, Emmeloord, where he was the ambassador for Braszat, a start-up club from Brasilia that was touring the Netherlands. On the touchline of the village green, Carlos Alberto cut an impressive, authoritative figure. Everyone still called him 'captain'. It was easy to understand why he was one of the few players who could reprimand and even scold Pelé or Gérson. You sensed he could snap at any moment.

I learned Portuguese, graduated from law school and J-School, and set out for Brazil. It wasn't always easy to chase players with a global status. It was as maddening as it was rewarding, an exercise in patience as most things in Brazil, and journalism, often are. Some players were always travelling, others were just not very connected. All of them had their own character traits: outspoken, bullish, intelligent, diplomatic, jovial, introverted, resentful, frustrated, generous, greedy. Almost all of them were nostalgic though, respectful of each other and critical of the modern game.

From the pristine beaches of Caraguatatuba, where I met Félix's daughter, to Batatais, the peaceful home of José Baldocchi, I criss-crossed Brazil, often on overnight buses after a dreary meal at a Graal roadside restaurant. In Rio, I staked out many hours at various radio stations to chat to Gérson, who, once you found him, became a chatterbox. On Copacabana beach, I played *futevolei*, a mix of football and beach volleyball, with Jairzinho. We shared beers, which softened him up.

My arts of persuasion were tested in different ways. Always out fishing, Brito rarely picked up the phone and, when he did, often after umpteen attempts a day, he sometimes pretended to be his own son. I never had the guts to tell him his voice was one of a kind. In Belo Horizonte, Tostão was very reluctant to talk at all at first.

The team's star remained unreachable. From the Morumbi stadium to Barnes & Noble in New York, I pursued Pelé. I tried to persuade the doorman at his downtown São Paulo flat. I befriended his brother-in-law and pleaded with Brazil's sports minister. I got his phone number when Pepe shared his address book. Nothing ever quite worked out.

All those journeys and interviews were crucial to enrich my understanding of Brazil and to ultimately tell the story of the 1970 team. This book doesn't attempt to describe every kick of the ball in Mexico, but rather to provide contextual analysis. The story stretches from 1963 to 1974 and describes the demise of Brazil's golden generation in 1966, the ensuing power struggles over the national team, João Saldanha's tempestuous coaching reign, the science behind the team and the Seleção's decline after 1970.

It was the eternal captain who got me hooked on Brazil and football in a way the modern game rarely can. Brazil's 1970 team remains an antidote to the mundane reality of the game today. After all, 'A thing of beauty is a joy forever.'

Sam Kunti, Leuven, 31 July 2022

Prologue

AT LAST, on 7 June 1970, the champions, both old and new, met. After all the hype, hysteria and hyperbole in the heat of Mexico's high-altitude Guadalajara, Brazil, the 1958 and 1962 World Cup winners, and England, the defending champions, were out to play a match that promised to stir the soul and marvel the mind.

The world, once again, fawned over the Brazilians. In their opening match, they had outclassed Czechoslovakia 4-1, reviving memories of some of the magic that had been lost since the finals in 1966. Brazil, despite conceding an 11th-minute goal, had crushed their opponents. Carlos Alberto Torres, the right-back and captain, recalled:

'It was a key moment. The first game always is. In the beginning, we were nervous as a team, but when Czechoslovakia scored the team woke up. It was a trigger to start playing the game we had envisaged and wanted to play.'

According to Rivellino:

'The adrenaline was ... The anxiety was huge. You just wanted to know what was going to happen right until the kick-off. I had levelled the score and Brazil opened with a marvellous 4-1 win. That's something that provided both calm and a boost. [I celebrated] you know, that way with my arms, swearing ...'

In the end, Brazil crucified the naive Czechs, who allowed their opponents so much space to explore, to roam in, and ultimately exploit. A wildly exuberant Brazil demonstrated virtuosity, artistry and exceeding flamboyance. Yet, Ladislav Petráš, Czechoslovakia's goalscorer, had exposed Brazil's characteristic insouciance at the back; the crucial flaw in the otherwise near-perfect disposition of the South Americans.

The England team, however, weren't impressed. They believed they could topple Mário Zagallo's team and that the Brazilian rearguard of goalkeeper Félix, Carlos Alberto, central defenders Wilson Piazza and Brito, and left-back Everaldo was suspect.

Piazza admitted:

'Obviously, in Brazilian football, there was concern about the defence. That wasn't just in the Seleção. The Brazilian press tolerated the playing formation with advanced wingers. Brazil play a 4-2-4 it was said, but at times it was 4-1-5 or 4-3-3. Zagallo was concerned and told us, you know, to stick to our positions.'

England, by contrast, seemingly wore a tactical straitjacket. As the celebrated 'Wingless Wonders', they had won the 1966 World Cup Final in a 4-4-2. Then, the impeccable Nobby Stiles screened the defence, allowing Bobby Charlton to attack through the centre. It was a tactic that, at the same time, cancelled out Franz Beckenbauer, the creative fulcrum of the German team. In Mexico, Alan Mullery, playing Stiles's role, along with both Martin Peters and Alan Ball, provided more steel, congesting Alf Ramsey's midfield. Bobby Charlton dropped deep from the attack. At 32, Charlton, the oldest outfield player in England's squad, was the linkman responsible for the team's attacking impetus.

Carlos Alberto explained:

'History made Brazil pre-tournament favourites, but the real favourites to win the World Cup going into the tournament were England. They were the defending champions and had an excellent team. They were more experienced than in 1966. England had Gordon Banks, Bobby Moore and Bobby Charlton. Brazil had to prove on the field that we were among the favourites. That's what we set out to do from the first game.'

Under Ramsey, England's football was practical in design and nature. Flair and flamboyance were dispensed with. Instead, the English coach valued doggedness, perseverance and commitment, all mundane qualities that had collectively seen them triumph in 1966. Four years later, Ramsey's view of football, and the world, had become more reductive. The English delegation was paternalistic and supercilious. Ramsey's ideas sometimes bordered on xenophobia.

Slightly aggrieved, Piazza recalled:

'England arrived and, in a way, it was natural – they, the English, arrived with a lot of pomp as if they were going to be champions. They even took along their own water. You also saw the Mexicans thinking, "The English are like *that*."'

'The winner of Brazil-England was always going to reach the final,' insisted Carlos Alberto. 'Everyone knew that. If you wanted to become world champions, you had to beat England!'

The contest was never going to be ordinary. The match, in part, shaped the outcome of the 1970 World Cup and defined Pelé's place in the pantheon of football gods. It also cemented Brazil's legacy in the global game.

'That game was decisive, the final *avant la lettre*,' said Jairzinho.

At least, that was the promise; a clash of cultures and different schools of football. England were a precision-engineered machine with a wellspring of energy and a rich seam of resolve, yet without flair in attack. Brazil, on the other hand, were the masters of the beautiful game albeit with a bumbling backline.

Piazza said:

'England played the way we had expected, marking well and with a strong mentality. They'd retained a good team from 1966, [and had] the credentials to chase another world title. Those guys were strong and tall, damn! And you wondered: how I am going to deal with them?'

The opening phase of play was circumspect, almost pedestrian, with England pacing themselves. They stroked the ball among themselves at an indecent canter. From the wings, their high crosses tested goalkeeper Félix's resolve and command over his penalty box. Jairzinho recalled:

'It was a very strategic game in which the two goalkeepers excelled like never before; Félix for Brazil and Banks for England. Félix was accustomed to it. Banks, I don't know if he had the habit of producing so many saves. It was a high-level game, a type of chess game. One team attacked, and the other one defended and then attacked [in return].'

Whenever Pelé moved into a dangerous position, his direct marker Mullery and England captain Bobby Moore beset him with almost pernickety precision, along with either left-back Terry Cooper or midfielder Bobby Charlton. Pelé was dispossessed twice but didn't flinch. He never did. The magnitude of the match didn't faze either talisman. They both played with stoic detachment and poise.

After ten minutes, the match ignited with a move of colossal vitality, a sign that Brazil, slightly stuttering at first, were beginning to assert themselves. The Brazilians' acceleration was almost devastating. Even

50 years later, the Brazil players remembered every nanosecond as if it were yesterday.

Carlos Alberto: 'Long pass to Jairzinho with the outside of the foot ...'

Jairzinho: 'I received the ball, dribbled past my marker Cooper and, from near the goal line, I crossed the ball towards the far post.'

Clodoaldo: 'Pelé had already seen Banks a bit out of position a few times and he had been waiting for a moment to strike. It is the most important lesson that I learned from Pelé; to have that different view of the game and the field.'

Carlos Alberto: 'When Pelé jumped, I began to celebrate – celebrate the goal.'

Jairzinho: 'There rose Pelé with his incredible thrust, heading downwards. But Banks, a quality goalkeeper with his velocity, explosiveness, flexibility and reflexes, was at the near post and got down and tipped the ball over.'

Gérson: 'It could only have been Banks because he had foreseen the save. Perhaps he expected it.'

Rivellino: 'My God, only players of that level would do what the two did! It was the perfect header. Banks thought the way Pelé did. When the ball bounced, if Banks would have tried to hold it, the ball would have passed him. It was like a volleyball play because he slapped the ball. He followed Pelé's thinking. It was an incredible move that required two geniuses.'

Chapter I

The Money Tour

PELÉ LIMPED in and out of matches, while the other demigods of Brazilian football hobbled along. Brazil's players were in a war of attrition. The matches, the travel, the functions, the receptions and the media obligations were taking their toll. They looked haggard, their tracksuits rumpled, their bodies sapped and, everywhere they went, opponents lurked with a weapons-grade enthusiasm to destroy the Seleção.

It was April 1963. In the space of 22 days, Brazil had criss-crossed the Old Continent playing nine friendly matches. 'We were simply on our last legs,' said Santos outside-left Pepe. The European tour was too exhausting. The reigning world champions lost four times but, according to the PR playbook of Brazil's all-powerful sports governing body, the Confederação Brasileira de Desportos (CBD), the tour was simply an experiment aimed at rebuilding the team in time for the 1966 World Cup in England.

'It was absurd, the truth is that the tour should have never happened,' fulminated Santos's Antonio Lima. Botafogo midfielder Gérson took the argument further to say that the ill-fated tour and its organisational template destroyed Brazil's chances of retaining the World Cup.

* * *

Brazil had just won the Copa Roca, a tournament with Argentina, and yet the mood in the Brazilian camp was sour in April 1963, the month São Paulo was to stage the fourth edition of the Pan-American Games, with the majestic Estádio Municipal Paulo Machado de Carvalho – the famous Pacaembu – as centrepiece venue. In the political arena, Brazilian president João Goulart was fighting for his survival.

The first leg of the European tour had resulted in an embarrassing 1-0 defeat against Portugal in Lisbon, nullifying the promise of a $500 bonus by João Mendonca Falcão, Brazil's delegation chief and the president of the Federação Paulista de Futebol (FPF), if the tour ended undefeated. The aggravation wasn't simply financial. Carlos Nascimento, the team's supervisor, and coach Aymoré Moreira, whose brother Zezé had coached Brazil at the 1954 World Cup, were having a squabble over personnel preferences against Portugal. The supervisor wanted to attack from the onset with Gérson in the starting line-up. The coach, however, leaned conservatively towards an unchanged team from the Argentina match-ups. The discordance was palpable and Brazil were left to lament a match that delivered very little, belying what the Portuguese press had billed as a 'theatrical spectacle'.

In 1962 the Brazilians had defended the World Cup against Czechoslovakia in Chile and, in the autumn, the Copa Libertadores champions Santos had enhanced Brazil's dominance in the game by wrestling the tag of best club in the world from Real Madrid. In the Intercontinental Cup, they defeated European champions Benfica 8-4 on aggregate. Europe and South America had a monopoly on the elite game and the Intercontinental Cup was established to crown the best team at club level. The competition was a matter of utmost importance and, in the second leg in Lisbon, Pelé destroyed Benfica. The scoreline was 5-2 in a match he still considers his finest. 'I believe that without exaggeration, without any exaggeration,' affirmed Benfica's José Augusto. 'Pelé was the light, the leading figure of the team, the best-ever Santos side. They were fabulous, extraordinary.'

In the spring of 1963 Brazil's national team carried their reputation, that of superlative ball virtuosos, who elevated the game to an art in a dazzling mix of speed, skill and precision to Europe. Portugal's coach José Maria Antunes warned Brazil that his team 'would play with a perfect defensive block in a 4-3-3 formation which won't allow penetration and not even long-distance attempts'. Antunes was a pragmatist but, in matching Brazil's system, he was audacious. After all, the Brazilians had won the last two World Cups perfecting that formation as Zagallo shuttled up and down his left wing to, in turn, offer defensive cover and attacking support. Portugal executed Antunes's game plan well, with defender Vicente shackling Pelé, who sustained an ankle injury in the 20th minute. The Portuguese and international press oscillated between euphoria and outright satire to describe how Vicente had closed down Pelé and marked him out of the game.

Alfredo Farinha from Portuguese sports daily *A Bola* asked, 'Where is Pelé? In Vicente's pocket!' Peter Lorenzo from the *Daily Herald* claimed that Vicente 'never allowed Pelé to distance himself more than 60cm from him'. And when Pelé did, Hernani Silva or Mario Coluna provided extra cover. The Portuguese rearguard disarmed Brazil's talisman. In attack, the constant movement off the ball from Augusto, Eusébio and Yauca confused the Brazilian defence.

After 20 minutes, the trio sensed that Brazil's left-back Altair lacked rhythm, so they channelled much of their attack on the right. Augusto scored. The experience was sobering for Brazil; they had no response to a well-organised block embedded in the successful system of their own design. The Brazilians were selfish in possession and guilty of poor decision-making. Their players often slowed down the pace and, in that respect, the second-half introduction of Zagallo was futile.

Altair, Claudio Danni, Dorval, Gérson, Pelé and Pepe, starters against Portugal, hadn't played in the World Cup Final in Chile, but Brazil's invincibility had been shattered. The aura of the double world champions suddenly shone a little less. Even in the pre-television age, Brazil was a byword for style and success. To watch Brazil play was to savour the greatness of single-name stars. It was to revel in the reality or even just the idea that they had no equals. It was as if each and every single one of their players were, in their own right, artists. Above all, Brazil possessed the ultimate thrill for a spectator: Pelé, the game's unmatched global superstar.

Europe remained besotted with the South Americans, and smitten with Pelé. Brussels was no different. The Belgian FA, the Koninklijke Belgische Voetbalbond, spent about 1.25 million Belgian francs in match fees and guest expenses to stage the first-ever encounter between Brazil and Belgium, considered a fair-to-middling European outfit.

* * *

In friendly matches, the Belgians were renowned as giant-slayers. In 1954, they were the first team to defeat world champions West Germany. The pertinacious striker Rik Coppens toyed with Werner Liebrich, the World Cup's best defender, to score the match's only goal. Belgium registered a more significant victory in 1956, winning 5-4 against Hungary, albeit the opposition were without both Nándor Hidegkuti and Zoltán Czibor. At the interval, Hungary led 3-1 but, in the second half, the ageing Hungarians were exposed. After the defeat, their coach Gusztáv Sebes was dismissed. Irrevocably, the decline of the Golden Team had begun. In just 90 minutes, the Belgians had wrecked a world order.

In 1963 Belgium were a light version of an accomplished Anderlecht team that, under the leadership of a blossoming Paul Van Himst, belonged to Europe's middle-tier clubs. The teenager was a youth product of the club and, in 1962, he won his first national crown with Anderlecht. The jaunty national team employed a 4-2-4 system, introduced by French coach Pierre Sinibaldi, who'd arrived at the Brussels club in 1960. A disciple of Albert Batteux, he imported the techniques from the French coaching school of Stade de Reims. It pleased Anderlecht's new president Albert Roossens, who'd outlined a policy of youth development and choice transfers to transform the club and achieve a style of play that would be branded 'champagne football'.

Van Himst became the focal point of a team that included local boys Jean-Marie Trappeniers, Pierre

Hanon, Jef Jurion and Jean Cornelis, Ostende duo Wilfried Puis and Laurent Verbiest, and Ronse's Jacques Stockman. Perhaps a young Van Himst with his agility, dribbles and instinct for goals reminded Sinibaldi of Raymond Kopa. Together they developed a slow, but skillful and polished game that resulted in the elimination of Real Madrid in the European Cup in 1962 after a 3-3 draw in the Spanish capital, followed by a 1-0 second-leg victory. Van Himst admitted that Madrid were 'a team on the way back' after their supremacy in the late 1950s but recalled how potent they still were. '[Alfredo] Di Stefáno was the first modern player, because he had a free role,' explained Van Himst. 'He could defend, attack and score goals. This was the Real Madrid of [Ferenc] Puskás, Di Stefáno and [Francisco] Gento. Di Stefáno had everything. Physically, he was unbelievably strong. He could just keep running.'

Players with a lot of lung power and pace were something of a problem for Anderlecht. In the Sinibaldi philosophy, the backline pushed up to use the offside trap and play possession football. That tenet left Anderlecht exposed against quick, counter-attacking teams. A hard-wired Dundee United eventually eliminated Anderlecht in the quarter-finals of that season's European Cup. 'Anderlecht was the first team to play that way [in Belgium],' said Van Himst. 'Standard was more about individual marking and physicality. It was based on Brazil, who also played 4-2-4 and the offside trap, which was dangerous against good teams. It taught us a lot. We also played in the opponent's half, because of Sinibaldi's approach.'

Jan Mulder, a 1965 Anderlecht recruit playing the Just Fontaine role, wrote of Sinibaldi that he was 'a nice guy, but not a special coach'. Van Himst dismissed that idea. 'That doesn't correspond with reality,' he insisted. 'Sinibaldi imparted something to our football. He was a nice guy, a Corsican, who had a lot of character. You had coaches who never looked at the human side of things, who neglected it. Not so for Sinibaldi. He was a figure with a lot of personality. His tactical approach was a point of discussion; the system with a flat back four, almost playing in the midfield, always with the offside trap. That helped us, but it was risky. Against Manchester United [in 1968] we dominated the match … We bettered Bobby Charlton and Nobby Stiles, but when they played diagonal passes in behind the defence they'd be one on one with the goalkeeper.'

Anderlecht went on to lose the tie 4-3 but, despite the flaws of Sinibaldi's system, 'champagne football' would become a part of the Anderlecht DNA and exert a major influence over the national team with a core of Anderlecht players in the early 1960s. 'The national team also played this way,' explained Van Himst. 'The limitation was that some Standard Liège players would be included and they were not accustomed to that system. You'd have instances when one would go forward while the other ran back.'

That's why on the eve of the match, Belgium's coach Arthur Ceuleers devoted a long team talk to tactics and how to stop Brazil's devastating frontline with zonal marking. Ceuleers's influence, however, was limited by technical director Constant Vanden Stock, who would become Anderlecht's chairman from 1971 to 1996, and called the shots in the selection committee. Faced with the presence of full-backs Jef Vliers from Standard Liège and Guy Raskin from Beerschot VAC, Ceuleers thought it inopportune to simply apply Sinibaldi's philosophy and play the Brazilians offside with a high defensive line.

His Brazilian counterpart also previewed changes, with Pelé in doubt after Vicente's knock. In Lisbon, the Brazilian team had demonstrated a prevalence to simply feed the ball to Pelé and wait for the talisman to play his way through the opponents but, under the close watch of Vicente, Pelé's moment of ignition never arrived.

Predictably, much of the build-up focused on Pelé and his injury. The Belgian newspaper *Het Volk* painstakingly noted that, upon arrival at Brussels airport, Pelé drank cold milk with his chicken Provençal. There was room for amusing observations as well as bigotry in the portrayal of Brazil as an exotic touring circus: '[Vicente] Feola, the fattest coach in the world, still ate with the same conviction of Sweden [the

World Cup] and Rome [the Olympic Games]. Dieting still seems unknown to him, because he devoured chunks of bread with tons of butter ... Mario Americo [the masseur] is still the same somewhat monkey-like type, a shoeblack somewhere in Chicago.'

With only 20 minutes until kick-off, Pelé was declared unfit; or perhaps he simply needed rest for the more prestigious friendly against France four days later in Paris. Belgium still faced seven world champions in goalkeeper Gilmar, defenders Djalma Santos, Mauro and Altair, midfielder Zito, and forwards Zagallo and Amarildo. Santos formed the backbone of the Brazilian team with five players; Mengálvio anchored the midfield alongside his club captain and Dorval played at outside-left.

On a night when Belgium showcased their own interpretation of the beautiful game in Brussels, Pelé's supporting cast was no match. The Belgians rendered Brazilian football outdated, outmoded and irrelevant. They played a rich, evocative game, exhibiting a mastery usually associated with their celebrated opponents. Within 21 minutes they'd scored four times. Belgium were practising blood sport. The attacking prowess of Stockman and the finesse of Van Himst stunned the Brazilian defence. It seemed the goalscoring would never stop. Together with Hanon and Paul van den Berg, the magic quartet ridiculed Brazil. Stockman, the archetypal Anderlecht forward with drive and lethalness inside the box, was the absolute star. After three minutes, he opened the score with a rasping shot and in the 12th minute he provided the assist from the left for Van Himst to double Belgium's lead with a first-time deflection beyond goalkeeper Gilmar.

Brazil were in disarray. They lacked mental sharpness, intensity and concentration. Flustered, they no longer played out of a calm and disciplined defence, which in normal circumstances would effortlessly interchange from 4-2-4 to 4-3-3. The third goal was even worse from Brazil's point of view, with Altair beating his own goalkeeper. The world champions were usurped from their own league, bewildered by Belgium's unexpected speed and precision. Stockman blasted a fourth past Gilmar. 'It was a shock,' said Pepe, who watched on from the bench. 'Moreira had replaced me with Zagallo, who defended more, but it didn't help.'

After all the pining for Pelé, the fans in the stands had forgotten about him. Instead, they were relishing the sight of the mighty Brazil being dismantled by a superb home team. In the 33rd minute, Altair cleared Van Himst's attempt off the line before Quarentinha, in a rare Brazilian attack, reduced the deficit to 4-1.

The match was no longer a contest after the interval. Around the hour mark, Stockman completed his hat-trick, displaying the full oeuvre of his skills by dribbling past three Brazilians before scoring. Djalma Santos, Altair and Mauro illustrated Brazil's impotence by repeatedly hoofing the ball long. 'Brazil didn't establish themselves at any point,' said Lima, who debuted against the Netherlands eight days later. 'The result, we felt, was a bit exaggerated, but altogether fair considering the football that Belgium had played.'

The final score read 5-1 and the Brazilians were embarrassed in a way that had some pondering the gravity of the result. In his daily column 'Na Grande Area' in *Jornal do Brasil*, star journalist Armando Nogueira lamented:

'It was at dusk on a Belgian Wednesday: the stars of deception were shining in the sky that adorned the Atomium monument, in Brussels. It was there, in the old Heysel Stadium, that I felt my body shiver ... I started to laugh – laughing out of shame. The men who organised this damned excursion degraded the Seleção and didn't rebuild the golden Seleção. Belgium is a modest team to demoralise the glorious legend of two admirable achievements of our football. The Belgians put the ball between the legs of the Brazilians – and the terraces sang the chorus of loud laughter. The Belgians exchanged back-heel passes – and the terraces still sang the chorus of loud laughter. Hardly did the Belgians know they were not defeating the golden team because we no longer have a golden team. The golden Seleção, the Belgians knew, never played to make money, the team of Didi only played for glory, the team of Vava played football so that the Brazilian people had more and more joy to be

Brazilian. The team of Nilton Santos can not be confused with this Seleção, crucified between an aeroplane and a tourist hotel.'

Inevitably, Belgian newspapers waxed lyrical. *Het Laatste Nieuws* exclaimed, 'Pelé played in our ranks!' *Le Soir* wrote of a 'démonstration éclatante' and *De Standaard* noted that the victory was a 'testimony to our football prosperity', but cautioned against reading too much into the result given Belgium's past disappointments in matches that mattered. Sweden and Switzerland had eliminated the Belgians in the 1962 World Cup qualifiers. 'At European level we did get results, but not enough in relation to the quality we possessed,' admitted Van Himst. 'We were semi-pros, something that played a part as well. We had a very good team, but perhaps we lacked a bit of professional guidance at the time. Everyone had a job, you know, a bit of office work.'

De Standaard did ponder the ramifications for Brazil and a shift in the balance of power:

'It will never be possible to accurately determine when an enterprise, a team or a career is over the top and when the downturn begins. England were humiliated in 1950 in Belo Horizonte by the football cowboys of the United States, but how long did it take for the British to drift from the level of the best European teams? Where did the decline of the renowned Hungarian phalanx from the first half of the fifties begin? In Bern?

In Istanbul? In Brussels? The absence [of Pelé and Garrincha] lifted the veil over the limitations of their successors. Brazil are still wearing football's crown, but their possibilities are no longer endless.'

Here, context is crucial. The result was of seismic significance for Brazil, but less so for the Belgians. Transient glory aside, the victory was largely inconsequential for Ceuleers's diffident semi-professional team. The 5-1 capitulation, Brazil's heaviest loss since the 1940 Copa Roca and the nadir of the tour, was insignificant in isolation, but subsequent defeats against the Netherlands (1-0) and Italy (3-0) exposed deeper issues.

* * *

The players offer differing explanations for Brazil's 1963 downturn. Amarildo had been instrumental in the 1962 World Cup win but he simply chuckled at the memory of the year that followed. The Brazilians went on a shopping spree around Europe, with a particular, if not unhealthy, interest in transistor radios and dolls. Amarildo told me:

'You know what it was like; there were few who travelled abroad. That tour was a stroll. Some players didn't train the way they had always trained. There was always a bit of freedom. It was football without any commitment. Well, we had obligations, yes. There was no camp [concentração]. When you play a game with nothing at stake, with no obligation to win … it was entertainment. The World Cup was valued. On tour, life was a bit more joyous and clearly the returns were very slim. It wasn't the Seleção of the World Cup. Everyone played, the balance was lost and the productivity diminished. These things happen, but better that it happens during the parties and the strolls than in the World Cup qualifiers or the World Cup. That would be different. It would be a different tour, a different way of approaching the games.'

'The Seleção in 1963 was disorganised, without a strong leadership,' said Gérson. That season, the midfielder moved from Flamengo to Botafogo. He'd debuted for the amateur national team at the 1959 Pan-American Games and represented Brazil at the 1960 Olympic Games in Rome but a knee injury prevented him from travelling to Chile. However, on the European tour he was still very much a novice, competing with Mengálvio for a role alongside Zito. The midfielder played three full matches on the tour: against Portugal, France and the Netherlands. But, while his vision and technique were already evident, he failed to strike up any connection with the Santos legend.

'You noticed the decline,' analysed Gérson. 'The disorganisation and the lack of physical fitness. There were some players from 1962. That would derail 1966. You could already picture what was going to happen. In

1963, in every game, it was a different team, as it would turn out to be in 1966. The disorganisation of the 1966 World Cup had its roots in that tour.'

Perhaps the minds of the Botafogo duo were drifting as well. Italian clubs were courting Gérson and Amarildo and, as early as Lisbon, Nascimento expelled representatives from both Juventus and Fiorentina from the team hotel. Amarildo's light-hearted explanation touches on a modicum of the truth, but Gérson's account is more instructive.

Strictly based on results, Brazil's tour was a disaster. In 56 matches from 1959 to 1963, the Brazilians had seen 40 wins, six draws and ten defeats. However, in the space of just 29 days and nine matches – 22 days in Europe as well as trips to Cairo and Tel Aviv – they were defeated four times. The end-of-tour victories over Egypt (1-0) and Israel (5-0) were irrelevant.

The selection committee panicked after the Belgian defeat, not helped by a 2-0 training-ground loss against Racing de Paris on the eve of the France friendly, which journalist Dacio de Almeida regarded as 'worse than ever' in *Jornal do Brasil*. Feola and Moreira were World Cup-winning coaches but their experience contributed little to a tour that should have been valedictorian for Brazil's golden generation. They didn't introduce a new generation either. The Seleção was in a transitional phase but there were some mitigating circumstances: the team's luminary Didi had retired and Garrincha was injured. In 1963, the Botafogo wizard with bendy legs played only two matches in a row. His knee was in a bad way, a splintered cartilage causing it to swell. Regular perforation and drainage did little to remedy the injury and, in 1964, surgery followed. Garrincha's desperately sad terminal decline had begun. In Europe, Moreira had a catchphrase about the inimitable winger: 'We should have brought Garrincha even if it was to play in a wheelchair.'

Feola also sidelined the 38-year-old Nilton Santos, Brazil's greatest-ever left-back, from his squad. São Paulo's Roberto Dias, Corinthians's Eduardo and Marcos as well as Santos's Lima and Rildo were debutants on the tour. Nevertheless, Feola had still retained 11 World Cup winners. 'You had players who couldn't be called up again and players who went for the first time,' explained Lima. 'All of this, instead of helping, was confusing.'

The team had just three run-outs before embarking for Europe. The tour diary was gruelling with little or no time to rest and recover in a schedule that compelled Brazil to play every three to four days.

'Eat, play, rest and recover as much as possible,' recalled Amarildo, in between all the tourism he'd undertake. Brazil even squeezed in a training match against a select team from Philips, the Dutch technology giant. All the players received a transistor radio and $100. That day the team arrived at midnight in Germany, where Falcão argued with German officials over the contractual details of a potential match in Berlin against a select of local players. He simply wanted more money. 'It was a Seleção *caça-níquel* [a gold-digging team],' lamented Lima. Rildo backed this up, going on to say that 'the CBD went on the tour to make money'.

* * *

Santos were the first Brazilian club to exploit their players, milking foreign tours for cash, almost on an industrial scale. In 1959, Santos and Pelé played 22 matches in 44 days in eight European countries, encountering, among others, Real Madrid, Barcelona, Hamburg, Feyenoord and Sporting Lisbon. That year Pelé played 82 matches for his club. A year later Santos scheduled a further 18 matches across Europe. This time in the space of 44 days. The 1961 tour was perhaps even tougher: 19 matches in 50 days. 'The workload and activity was intense,' remembered Lima, who played for Santos from 1961 to 1971. 'We disputed the Paulista championship, the Rio-São Paulo tournament, the Copa Libertadores and toured. You never stopped. You played nearly the whole year.'

The Brazilian club became football's equivalent of the Harlem Globetrotters and the CBD had no qualms about replicating Santos's exploitative model. Pelé was the standout player, a global brand and a magic money machine all in one. A lucrative business was built around his personality.

At least Nascimento kept up the pretence. He never ceased to repeat how important the tour was in building a fresh team for the 1966 World Cup. Before the tour's first match, he rued the absence of so many great players. 'Unfortunately, it is necessary to renew the team and let's hope that the new players reach the heights of the old ones who will never be forgotten; Nilton Santos, Zozimo, Didi, Bellini, Vava and Castilho,' said Nascimento. 'Only those who lived with these guys, like me, understand their true value. It is sad they are not part of the touring party, but we are obliged to rebuild … if we do not want to transform the dream of conquering the World Cup into a pure mirage.'

On tour the players received a bonus of $100–$200 for each win. 'They gave Pelé a bit more, which was about $50,' said Rildo. The CBD's net profit from the match fees, ticketing and sponsoring, revealed CBD president João Havelange, was estimated to be $250,000. After Lima and Eduardo had left the field in tears following the 1-0 defeat to the Netherlands, *Jornal dos Sports'* columnist Fernando Horacio wrote that they weren't to blame, in a column titled 'Exploiters Don't Cry'.

Havelange was a rising star in sports administration, who prided himself on never entering a dressing room. Having participated in two Olympic

Games, first as a swimmer and then as a water polo player, he had an upright, athletic posture and was an imposing personality. His full name Jean-Marie Faustin Godefroid de Havelange revealed an aristocratic, Belgian ancestry. In 1963 he became a member of the International Olympic Committee (IOC). At the CBD, Havelange's management strategy had always been risky. He relied on loans and public funding to offset any deficits. Financial limitations, Havelange believed, weren't enough to constrain his expansive agenda to develop amateur sports across the board and to improve Brazil's medal haul at the Olympic Games.

In Rome, at the 1960 Olympic Games, 81 athletes, Brazil's largest delegation ever, represented the country. In the 100m freestyle swimming competition, Manoel dos Santos claimed bronze. The basketball team matched him. Arguably, the 39th rank in the medal table, alongside British West-Indies, was a modest result, but this time around Brazilian athletes had enjoyed better conditions to prepare because of the substantial investment in their disciplines. With its nationwide popularity, it was football that funded the other sports.

The returns of the 1962 World Cup win were, however, limited and Brazil's plummeting economy and subsequent inflation, the consequences of overheated national-developmentalism from the Juscelino

Kubitschek era, led to a financial crisis at the CBD. Havelange needed money. The CBD invested in real estate on one of Rio de Janeiro's main avenues, the Rio Branco. The prize asset, however, remained the national team, so in the spring of 1963 they were sent on a money tour, even if it meant forfeiting participation in the South American championship. The fundraising tactic wasn't novel. In 1960 Brazil played Egypt thrice in Cairo, on the invitation of popular president Gamal Nasser, raising $15,000.

In 1963 Brazil broke multiple records in Europe. Gate receipts in Hamburg were $24,190, a German record, and £80,000 in London, an English record. At Wembley, Brazil met Alf Ramsey and a young Bobby Moore for the first time. In the 85th minute, Bryan Douglas prevented the hosts from losing one of that year's FA centenary celebration matches with a tap-in at the far post.

Upon appointment, Ramsey had assumed all selection responsibilities. Brazil's unwieldy selection committee of Moreira and Feola, on the contrary, remained flustered. 'You had two coaches, how could they even be expected to build a team?' asked Rildo. 'They were questioning each other. Aymoré [Moreira] wanted a player, Feola another. So, that was part of the disorganisation of the Seleção. Aymoré managed one way, Feola the other. When the Seleção returned home, Aymoré was dismissed. The two didn't understand each other. He'd say A and the other B. They were never in tune as two coaches of Brazil should be.'

They resolved to field as many Santos players as possible. With the entire squad fit for once, a Santos-heavy Brazil defeated Sepp Herberger's West Germany 2-1 in Hamburg, arguably their finest outing on the tour, before drawing with England. In Milan, however, Italy swept a Santos-styled Brazil aside, 3-0. Gilmar claimed that Falcão asked team doctor, Hilton Gosling, to forcefully inject Pelé's knee before the Italy match. 'Falcão sent Gosling, but Pelé didn't accept the injection,' said Rildo. '[Giovanni] Trapattoni neutralised Pelé for 90 minutes. Pelé didn't do anything in that game. They wrote that Trapattoni stopped Pelé in his footsteps, but the problem was that Pelé was so tired.'

'Santos's team understanding couldn't simply be copied,' said Lima. 'That was among us. There was a lot of criticism in Brazil at the number of players from Santos. They selected nine players from Santos and two or three players from the other clubs, who were going to form the starting eleven. Did it work out? No! The Brazilian press criticised the tour with reason: the players were worn out from the state championships and then you come up with a tour to take on Germany, Italy and England.'

Amid all the confusion, chaos, tourism, exhaustion and greed, which played an insidious role throughout the tour, the Brazilians failed to realise that European football was changing. Portugal and the Netherlands marshalled defensive blocks, Belgium relied on skill, and Italy mixed organisation with technique. Indeed, there was no anointed formula to beat Brazil, but each team trusted their own virtues. Europe's game was slowly gaining in strength and physicality.

Lima maintained:

'The big problem wasn't them, the big problem was us. Falcão was invited as delegation boss. Here comes the proof that there was an understanding between Mendonca Falcão, the president of the FPF, and João Havelange, the president of the CBD. There was an agreement; you take so many Paulista players and some Carioca players and you form the Seleção, and let's play 10 or 15 games and pocket the money. Done! I am not going to use the word exploited, but it was a tour based upon the players of Santos. Why would you take nine players from Santos? You are basically selecting the entire team. Why? To sign the most lucrative contracts.'

Falcão's role on tour was ceremonial. However, his various positions at home suggested that he was a *cartola*: Portuguese for top hat and a colloquialism in Brazil for a powerful football official. He ran one of Brazil's most powerful state football federations, sat on the CBD, presided over the Conselho Nacional de Desportos, the country's national council for sports, and even dabbled in politics. The tour was a tit for tat – the prestige of heading the Seleção in exchange for his loyalty. This arrangement suited Falcão, and his position in São Paulo remained protected even if Paulo Machado de Carvalho, a football official at São Paulo FC and the owner of TV Record, yielded immense power. On tour, Falcão, in his own right, managed to organise an audience with Pope John XXIII through the Brazilian Embassy in Rome.

According to Rildo:

'All of us, the players, knew that the CBD travelled for money. The CBD had a financial interest. All the players noticed this, but they couldn't do anything. The only one who could have possibly changed something was supervisor Carlos Nascimento, but he didn't do it, because it was in his own interest not to. The players didn't have the physical condition to even play 30 minutes. In the first half, we'd play more or less, but in the second half we were just dead. Even against Egypt we had problems. It was difficult. Egypt were shit, but we all wanted to be substituted and we didn't have the physical condition to finish the game. It was a disastrous tour, one of the worst Brazil had ever undertaken, it was said at the time.'

Brazil were rushing headlong into a crisis and didn't heed the warning signs. On the eve of the France match, Dr Gosling remarked that just three or four players in the entire squad were match fit. A fortnight after the tour, he warned that, without proper physical preparation, Brazil wouldn't retain the World Cup in

1966. In fact, he said, 'Brazil will lose the next World Cup if we do not seek to improve our players' physical preparation because the Europeans for reasons that include race, nutrition, medical care and the weather are currently playing a vigorous and fast-paced game that we can't cope with.'

Did the doctor's warning really matter in the end? Brazil and Santos had found a financial fail-safe. At the time of Dr Gosling's foreboding, Santos, with Pelé as a busker, were on the road yet again, playing against the likes of Eintracht Frankfurt on a tour that would stretch for 28 days and culminate with a tournament in Milan, alongside Rio de Janeiro club Flamengo.

The circus was simply moving on.

Chapter II

The Circus

WHEN WAS it over, exactly? At what point did Brazil relinquish their global crown, first won in 1958 and then retained in 1962? There came a moment in the first-round match of the 1966 World Cup in England, sometime between Mário Coluna's 27th-minute goal and Eusébio's 85th-minute strike that, no matter what Brazil did, no matter how they tried, they weren't going to defeat a magnificent Portugal. A few days earlier, a 3-1 defeat against Hungary had been even more telling. Perhaps Brazil had simply exhausted any hopes of defending their world title long before they arrived in England.

'Did the players indulge in the idea of Brazil as the football nation in the run-up to the 1966 World Cup?' I asked Antonio Lima at a sun-drenched Vila Belmiro in 2019. He replied, 'Brazil needed to win a first World Cup, in 1958, to be taken seriously. The title defence [in 1962] was simply a confirmation.'

After Brazil's first World Cup win, Nelson Rodrigues, the playwright and great chronicler of the Brazilian game, argued that the nation could discard the 'mongrel complex'. He wrote: 'No one is still ashamed of his nationality. The people no longer judge themselves as mongrels. The Brazilian has a new image of himself; now he sees himself in the generous totality of his immense virtues.' His conclusion that the 1958 victory 'taught that the Brazilian, whether he wants it or not, is the best' was as dramatic as it was delusional. He was often guilty of dangerous hyperbole, asserting that 'the pure truth is this; any Brazilian player, when he sheds his inhibitions and puts himself in a state of grace, is unique, in terms of fantasy, improvisation and invention. To sum up – we have an excess of gifts.'

In one clean sweep, he dismissed the *Maracanazo*, Brazil's traumatic defeat in the 1950 World Cup at the hands of neighbours Uruguay, as a cause for Brazil's inferiority complex. His world view was nationalistic and antagonistic – Brazil against Europe and the colonisers – but Brazil's supremacy was assured if the Brazilian believed in himself. His thinking was a product of his time, steeped in the fascist views of Getúlio Vargas, who built the *Estado Novo* from 1937 to 1945. Vargas modernised and developed Brazil by incorporating the emerging popular classes in society while leaving the quasi-feudal hierarchy untouched.

By the mid-1950s, Brazil was thriving and well on the way to a glorious destiny. On the back of Vargas's policies, the charismatic President Juscelino Kubitschek, elected in 1955, committed himself to Brazil's super-acceleration, predicated on his 'fifty years progress in five' programme. On deserted scrubland in what was considered the *interior*, he christened a new national capital, Brasilia. Architect and urban planner Lucio Costa designed the city in a shape suggesting an aeroplane; Oscar Niemeyer furnished the nascent capital with sinuous and sensual buildings, renowned as distinguished expressions of *Brasilidade*. It was a time of bloom with bossa nova and footballing hegemony.

Kubitschek and, later, João Goulart envisioned a more egalitarian society, but as the tanks rolled down Rio de Janeiro's streets in May 1964, establishing a military junta, supported by the US government, the dream was short-lived. Brazil's democratic experiment ended abruptly.

The national team, however, remained a powerful export product. The Seleção was deemed almost invincible. At the end of March 1966, coach Vicente Feola took the idea of the football nation to an extreme when he called up a 45-man preliminary squad for the World Cup in England. Ten survivors from the 1963 European tour remained. In 1958, Feola had nominated 33 players; in 1962 his successor Moreira expanded the party to 41 players. Even to a layman, the arsenal of 40 outfield players and five goalkeepers seemed excessive.

What, if any, criteria was Feola using to justify his choices? He drew from a list of 75 players; Nascimento, a member of the selection committee, from 70 players. 'Too bad that we can't call up 90 players to show the world our strength,' said team doctor, Dr Gosling, at the end of the four-hour meeting.

The bloated squad was the result of guesswork, compromise and politics. In the background, a boardroom conflict between Havelange and Paulo Machado de Carvalho over who would head the Brazilian delegation had festered for weeks. The former São Paulo official wanted Moreira returned to the backroom staff; Havelange, on the other hand, firmly backed Feola. The pair fell out, leading to Paulo Machado's resignation.

The Brazilian press relished the spat, with extensive coverage. Their narrative, however, was flawed. Havelange was accused of being jealous of Paulo Machado's prior successes in both 1958 and 1962, but the two football officials were perfect allies. A powerful media executive, Paulo Machado's interests were limited to his own little kingdom, São Paulo. For many years, Paulo Machado had fended off demands from the FPF and local clubs to pay for broadcast rights.

In 1965 the dispute reached the legislature in Brasilia. In response, Paulo Machado sought support from the Mayor of São Paulo, Faria Lima, falling back on *Lei* 4,007, which regulated the transmission of sporting events in municipal stadiums without the obligation to pay anything to the clubs. 'We defend the rights of millions of TV spectators, the clubs of 160,000 members,' boasted Paulo Machado. The clubs, led by São Paulo FC President Laudo Natel, didn't budge and, in retaliation, staged matches at the Morumbi stadium, a move that alienated Paulo Machado, who once was the strongman at the Morumbi club himself.

Paulo Machado wasn't a threat to Havelange, who wanted to conquer the world. In the 1958 and 1962 World Cups, he'd delegated all responsibility to Paulo Machado, then the boss of the Brazilian delegation. It was his insurance policy: a win would reflect well on the CBD president, but a defeat would exonerate him. In 1966 Havelange arrogated the position because this time he wanted the glory. Brazil, he firmly believed, were poised for a record third World Cup win. 'No one, in his mind, would defeat Brazil, with the quality of players available,' said Rildo.

The backroom staff was also split. Corpulent, Feola's health was deteriorating; the exact reason why Moreira had replaced him for the 1962 World Cup. His heart was in a precarious state. Perhaps he was too busy scouting players to dwell on dietary considerations. The rumours about Feola's coronary problems remained alarming and he was sometimes seen catnapping on the bench, attested Rildo. 'Vicente Feola hardly talked, he was very quiet,' said Paulo Henrique. 'It was mostly [trainer] Paulo Amaral, who gave the instructions.'

In reality, it was Nascimento who was the hands-on ruler of the team. Nascimento and Feola never truly attacked each other head-on but the discordance slowly undermined the team's stability. 'Feola carried out Nascimento's orders,' said Rildo. 'On the bench, he was a fictional figure.'

'At the time, a coach was conversational, easy-going, an adviser and your friend,' explained Tostão, whose Brazil debut came against Chile in the Copa Bernardo O'Higgins on 15 May 1966. 'Feola was a good man, a big father figure, but he didn't have any great strategic knowledge at all. He was a person of his time, but it wasn't just him: [most] coaches were like that, you know?'

Feola was a bon vivant, a cross between an epochal coach and an uncle everyone liked. 'He won you over with his friendship,' said striker Silva Batuta, who played under him at São Paulo in the late 1950s.

Austere and cocky, Nascimento had returned in 1966 as the right-hand of Havelange, but the ensuing political machinations dismantled his invaluable relationship with Paulo Machado. 'Nascimento was the *Cacique Branco*, the white boss,' said midfielder Denilson.

The one thing Havelange, Feola and Nascimento didn't disagree on was squad selection. They were convinced that the past guaranteed a fail-safe for yet more success, picking twice world champions Gilmar, Djalma Santos, Bellini, Zito, Garrincha and Pelé as well as Orlando and Dino Sani, both 1958 world champions, and Altair, 1962 world champion. They'd been good servants, and Feola, along with the CBD, wanted to honour the veterans with a valedictory tournament and an assumed third world title. Paulo Henrique, who has the physique of an impressive, young boxer but with lustrous white hair, lamented: 'They went as a reward.'

With three months until their World Cup opening match against Bulgaria in July, Paulo Henrique and the Brazilian team boarded a bus to Lambari in Minas Gerais, one of four cities alongside Caxambu, Teresopolis and Serra Negra to host the Brazilian squad. Back in 1958 Brazil's preparation stretched for two months and eight days; in 1962 they added two days.

The 1966 squad was spoiled with so much time to prepare but the training camp was soon plagued by acts of prolonged dilettantism. Lambari, Caxambu, Teresopolis and Serra Negra were provincial spa towns, replete with honeymooners, geriatric tourists and those desperate for a cure. Nothing usually ever happened there, so the locals feted football's heroes. They celebrated their sojourn and saluted their impending victory in England, with all too much zeal. Lambari organised cocktail soirees, a flyover by the air force, a special mass and a boat show. That incensed Caxambu, which staged banquets, school parades and other public spectacles to wow the delegation and upstage their neighbours.

At practice, however, the supporters jeered. Feola (who'd slowly gained the moniker 'Fatso') and Nascimento reacted angrily but they found even less tranquillity in Teresopolis, a cool enclave in the mountains north of Rio de Janeiro. There the hype around the Seleção went into overdrive. Speaking from a podium, the town's Mayor Flavio Bortoluzzi welcomed the squad, accompanied by the rehearsed tunes of the local marching band and the contortions of Horacio, an amateur trapeze artist. Havelange received the city's honorary citizenship. Bemused, the players shuffled on to the stage for the requisite photo-op. They headlined the parade, an exercise in gratuitous nation-building and self-gratification. 'It was as if we had already won the World Cup,' lamented Rildo. 'The CBF ordered the parades.'

'It was the politicking linked to the CBD,' recalled Tostão. 'There were political interests to play in certain places and to train in some cities. Brazil was going through a very big transition, turning into a technocracy. The CBD was on good terms with the government and the military.'

Admiral Heleno de Barros Nunes and Brigadier Jerônimo Bastos were part of the CBD's coterie. The admiral, a Vasco da Gama fan, happily partook in the organisation and attended luncheons. He'd become CBD president in 1975. In 1969 his brother, Adalberto, became the Navy Minister in the administration of General Emílio Garrastazu Médici.

His unquestionable talent aside, Tostão was an inadvertent benefactor of the political game. In 1920 Ismael Alvariza became the first player who didn't ply his trade in either Rio de Janeiro or São Paulo to feature for the national team. He roamed on the left wing for his club Brasil de Pelotas in Rio Grande do Sul, Brazil's most southerly state. Yet for decades the two main states remained football's centre of gravity, privileged due to abundant human resources.

In the 1960s, both Santos and Botafogo built dynasties, competing time and again for the crown of Brazil's best team and exporting their exuberant brand of football around the world. The duopoly was never disputed. In December 1966, however, Cruzeiro won the Taça Brasil, a precursor to the national championship, against Santos. In Belo Horizonte, Cruzeiro destroyed the planet's best XI 6-2. At half-time, the Minas club, playing with lightning-quick transitions, led 5-0. Walking off to the dressing room, defensive midfielder Wilson Piazza glanced over at the scoreboard and stared in disbelief. The scoreline was surreal. He was marking

Pelé out of the match. Cruzeiro were organised in a nominal 4-3-3 with Dirceu Lopes and Tostão alongside Piazza in the midfield, but the former two were often bombing forward, leaving Piazza single-handedly in the holding role in a 4-1-5. 'Like Garrincha, Pelé was considered unmarkable,' explained Piazza. 'I had to show that I was a Pelé without the ball. When he built up play, I had to destroy play.'

Still, at the interval, Piazza wasn't convinced of victory. Their opponents were, after all, Santos. Nothing was insurmountable for coach Lula's team. Santos rallied with two goals from Toninho Guerreiro before Dirceu Lopes tapped in a sixth for Cruzeiro. Infuriated, Pelé, refusing to accept defeat, was sent off. 'I pulled my leg out of the way at the very last minute or he would have broken it,' said Piazza. 'The referee Armando Marques said, "Off, mister Edson!"'

In the return leg, Cruzeiro needed only a simple draw to win the Taça Brasil. Instead, they won again, 3-2. Cruzeiro, the champions of Minas Gerais, became a club with national appeal. Lyrical journalists crowned Tostão the 'new Pelé', a sobriquet that left the Cruzeiro player bewildered.

In Tostão's view, his inclusion in the 1966 World Cup squad, along with Nado from Pernambuco's Nautico and Alcindo from Rio Grande do Sul's Grêmio, was intended 'to appease the states'. In a tense climate, punctuated by tribalism, the Federação Mineira de

Futebol, the football federation of Minas Gerais, as well as local clubs and students launched a campaign, aptly named '*Tostão na Seleção, não tem apelação: o tri é nosso*' (Tostão in the team needs no second thoughts: the third title is ours).

Brazil's first *coletivo* in Lambari was a run-out to satisfy the local authorities and the kick-off to a maddening and corrosive sequence of practice matches marked by confusion, indecision, injuries and, naturally before a World Cup, endless petty conjecture. Players were divided into four, colour-coded teams that criss-crossed Minas Gerais and Rio de Janeiro to play against insignificant opponents from insignificant towns, Esportiva de Guarantingueta, Tupi, Bangu and São Bento de Sorocaba. At times, the blue team played in white shirts. Pelé anchored the red team and, thus, the first XI of Gilmar, Carlos Alberto, Bellini, Orlando, Rildo, Zito, Gérson, Jairzinho, Servilio and Parada.

'The first training in Lambari was on a Sunday,' recalled Rildo. 'In the first half, the white shirts played the green ones and in the second half it was the blue team against the yellow team. You see we had four teams, how was that possible?'

The nomadic nature of the training camp, along with the bloated squad, excused any hopes of normality. Nevertheless, the CBD and Havelange weren't alarmed. There was always something to be gained, or at least more profit to be made. In an age without the riches of multi-million sponsorship deals or broadcast revenues, the CBD often complained about being short of money. With an anticipated World Cup expenditure of CrS 1.7 billion, the governing body sourced funds to the tune of CrS 2 billion, mostly from gate receipts, the national lottery and the federal budget. The confederation also invested CrS 1.4 billion in a new headquarters.

The host cities acted as benefactors. Governor Israel Pinheiro budgeted $6,500 for Lambari to host the Seleção. The city of Teresopolis covered all of the team's expenses. With star players often injured on the touchline, Admiral Heleno Nunes was sometimes complaining about a drop in gate receipts from the training matches. 'It should never have come down to a city offering something,' said Lima. 'In exchange for what? To please A, B or C?'

'It all got off to the wrong start, with the CBD removing Paulo Machado,' recalled Paraná. 'The Rio faction had the team train to please everyone.'

Assistant physical trainer Rudolf Hermany, a judo coach and a relative of Havelange, even recommended the players be taught how to fall. In hindsight, Rildo ridiculed the idea, singling out the physical trainer's background as a critical mistake. He said, 'From the age of 16, 17 a player understands how to fall and get up again. Hermany didn't understand the game.'

The players were unsettled. They were stuck in a seemingly endless holding pattern, consumed by a single question: who would be dropped next? Each and every new match filled each player with fresh doubts.

'We were restless [and] the anxiety!' remembered Denilson. 'Gosh, will I be a starter or not? Your head wanted to rest at night. I was consumed by the idea that I couldn't be axed – I can't be axed! Horrible, horrible.'

I met Denilson in 2019 at the office of the Associação Nacional dos Servidores da Polícia Federal (Association for Pensioners of the Federal Police) in downtown Rio de Janeiro. Dressed in a white T-shirt and black jeans, he was unassuming, mild-mannered and very thoughtful. He pursued a career in law enforcement after leaving the game. He was one of Brazil's first and most classic holding midfielders, *cabeça de area*. He understood the game from the goal line to the halfway line, covering the back, marking tightly and dispossessing any opponent. His passing and distribution of the ball were unsophisticated but, even if his role wasn't glamorous at all, Denilson captained Fluminense for the vast majority of his spell from 1964 to 1973 in Laranjeiras. He was one of the first black captains at the elite club. Fluminense's nickname is 'rice-powder' (*po-de-arroz*), which up to the 1950s the club's black players literally used to lighten their skin before playing. In the 1960s it seems, however, that Denilson never confronted the issues of racism, perhaps as a means of protecting himself.

'My captaincy led to the end of certain preconceptions because Fluminense were *po-de-arroz* and I, with my colour, wore the armband,' said Denilson. 'Racism existed in Brazil. You sensed that, but I just had to swallow it because I was the captain. You couldn't cover everyone's mouth in the stands. When you know that there is racism, it is not worth arguing. You swallow it and you leave it alone. It never affected me. Racists are sick and repressed.'

In 1966 Denilson was one of the more than 40 mortals who agonised for weeks over his chance of playing in the World Cup. Pelé, with his sterling credentials, didn't need to worry. He was exempt from speculation. He was never going to be omitted from the final squad. 'In training, you'd watch which shirt Pelé was wearing,' stressed Denilson.

'Comical!' said Batuta. 'If Pelé wore blue and you didn't, you were axed, tchau!'

After weeks of demonstrative excellence and consistency in training, Gérson was also a shoo-in, but the other players remained subject to the whims and prevaricating of the selection committee. 'Your head was spinning,' said Paulo Henrique, whose inclusion in the blue team left him on the fringes and vulnerable.

'After 20, 25 minutes of training in the first team, you would simply be substituted,' added Lima. 'You didn't get any explanation as to why.'

On the right wing, Jairzinho, 21, was competing against his idol Garrincha, Paulo Borges and Nado. As a teenager, he'd watched Garrincha both train and play at the Rua General Severiano, Botafogo's training complex, an opportunity he relished. Garrincha was a magician. He confounded twice over with exactly the same trick: a step-over, the feint and the acceleration past his direct opponent. He fooled both the opposition and the fans, whose raucous laughter at so much ingenuity filled the stands. Amused, they watched him over and over again, and whenever he sped down the touchline they wondered: how did he do that? His physiognomy remained a mystery but they revelled in his relentless mockery of full-backs.

'He was the Charlie Chaplin of football,' testified Botafogo star Paulo Cézar Lima (Caju), who watched a peak Garrincha train. 'You don't have to explain Charlie Chaplin. You simply laugh. With Garrincha, it was the same thing. He was like a bird, flying and dribbling everyone. What a show! At training. Against Russia, against Colombia, against Madureira. Against anyone. It didn't matter.'

At 32, Garrincha was playing for Corinthians in São Paulo; or at least pretending to. His body was ravaged by his 1964 knee operation, his alcoholism and the toll of his tempestuous personal life. After the 1962 World Cup Final, Garrincha didn't feature for Brazil for three years and injury prevented him from participating in the 1964 Nations Cup. In June 1965 he returned, no longer with his dizzying dribble, great speed and wonders of improvisation, in a grudge match, a 5-0 demolition of Belgium at the Maracanã.

In 1966 he arrived for Brazil's training camp in no fit state, with a wrecked knee and three-centimetre atrophy in his right leg, which according to Dr Gosling wasn't 'an unsolvable clinical problem'. He devised a personalised training programme for Garrincha with 20kg weights, iron shoes and electrotherapy. His attempt to revitalise Garrincha was folly. 'Garrincha was no longer the Garrincha that we knew,' said Rildo, who played with him between 1962 and 1965 at Botafogo.

Flamengo's Paulo Henrique encountered Garrincha early in his career. The secret of marking the wizard with bent legs was simple. 'Never allow him on the ball first!' exclaimed Paulo Henrique. What if Garrincha did get to the ball first? 'If he turned, you couldn't dispossess him and he'd toy with you,' admitted Henrique. 'Flávio Costa taught me to watch the ball at his feet, and not to watch his body. It is the ball that moves. Keep watching the ball or he'll destroy you.'

But in 1966 Garrincha often stood with the ball at his feet, sometimes in anguish, sometimes clueless, simply looking to pass it on. His dribbles no longer ridiculed opponents; his accelerations were no longer devastating. His spontaneity and fantasy were deserting him. 'His signature move was to have the ball at his feet,' said Paulo Henrique. 'He'd feign and you'd get beaten, you'd chase him. He'd turn back and he'd do it all over again. He had lost that. At times during practice I told him to dribble past me! "Go, go this way!" Pum, I'd take the ball from him! He no longer had the strength; his knee didn't help either.'

To compensate for his lack of fitness, Garrincha shifted his style of play: he no longer wanted to receive the ball at his feet but ran in behind his marker more often. 'The press wrote that Garrincha was out of shape in two or three training sessions,' said Rildo. 'They said that I marked him well, but the problem was that Garrincha didn't have that sprint, that acceleration anymore. Instead, I said: "It is just training, he isn't even bothering."'

'Mané's strength was his burst of speed and when he lost that he lost the condition to play football, because his genius, even inside Mané's own head, was that explosiveness,' said Batuta.

'He shouldn't have been around [in 1966],' said Gérson.

Garrincha was the sad symbol of a generation in steady decline, one that shouldn't have been considered for reselection. Feola's insistence on dragging the veterans and their star power along hastened Brazil's own doom. The coach's inertia was alarming. Feola was often inconspicuous, his quiescence almost a matter of personal policy. When he did speak, a dangerous gap opened up between his firm statements and meek inaction. His passivity and Nascimento's false pretences over the team's progress were small but devastating steps in Brazil's failure to form a proper first XI.

A simple mathematical exercise corroborated the startling irrationality of selecting 40 players and five goalkeepers. In his preferred 4-2-4 formation, Feola could form at least 13,063,680 different teams. 'We would get to the year 2000 without ever exhausting the combinations,' wrote Nogueira poignantly, the day after AC Milan's Amarildo arrived from Italy to complete the squad as 46th member and expand Feola's matrix.

Seleção A and Seleção B replaced the red, blue, white and green teams when international opposition arrived halfway through May. Both national teams were intertwined, representing the same flag, wearing the same CBD crest, and yet they often played in different cities against rotating opposition.

One question invariably evoked another. Who featured in the first team? Did Feola apply a 4-2-4 or 4-3-3? Why were the players still in such deplorable physical condition? Who would partner Pelé in the attack? The chaos multiplied. After six weeks of training, Brazil were no closer to a starting XI. The defence was a metaphor for Brazil's confusion and paralysis. Djalma Santos, Djalma Dias, Altair and Paulo

Henrique replaced the preferred backline of Carlos Alberto, Brito, Orlando and Rildo in a friendly against Poland. No one understood Feola's and Nascimento's opaque thinking; not the media, not the fans and, least of all, the players. 'You no longer knew who you were!' exclaimed Lima.

In May, on the exact same day that he arrived from Italy at the training camp, Inter Milan's Jair da Costa, the 47th squad member, was dropped with an injury, alongside six other fringe players. After all the haggling between the CBD and the Italian club over Da Costa's release, this outcome was disappointing and predictable: foreign-based players were barred from the national team. At 40 players, the squad was still colossal. The selection committee pretended to be proactive but, in reality, they just maintained the status quo.

In June, Nascimento pruned the squad to 27 players. Carlos Alberto was axed alongside Djalma Dias and 11 others. Dias claimed the choice for Bellini was motivated by nostalgia. Carlos Alberto had played 720 minutes in 25 practice matches, the most of any of the dropped players. A year earlier, Nascimento had also been responsible for Carlos Alberto's exit at Fluminense. The right-back moved to Santos. 'Feola opted for Djalma Santos and Fidelis of Bangu instead,' said Carlos Alberto. 'I had been in the senior team, training and playing exhibition games before the team was to head to England. It was a shock.'

'The greatest right-back of all time was not even selected for the Seleção!' Rildo said in exasperation. 'If you had blended Fidelis and Djalma Santos, that player would not have reached Carlos Alberto's ankles.'

Interdependent, the players shared a destiny, but navigating Feola's selection purgatory demanded self-discipline, patience and mental fortitude. Inevitably, the players' competitive nature sowed some degree of discord and mild distrust. The players became prone to forming cliques. 'There was a little group here and a little group there,' said Paraná, who'd hang out with Tostão and Alcindo. 'It wasn't united.'

Brazil arrived in England with one of the oldest squads. They had the oldest captain and the oldest player in the tournament. Near the end of their careers, Gilmar, the finest goalkeeper of his generation, Bellini, the 1958 World Cup-winning captain, and Djalma Santos, a pioneer of all-round modern full-backs, could no longer match the athletic development of the game. They lacked the stamina to play consecutive World Cup matches. The fading Zito didn't play a single minute in England because of a niggling injury. Feola and his veterans no longer suited the moment.

'It was the illusion that players who had won would win again; that experience superseded technique and form,' said Tostão.

Chapter III

The Elimination

PERHAPS BY 1966 Brazilian expectations had also become unreasonable and untenable: winning the World Cup was an obligation to prove the nation's success on the global stage. In Feola's squad selection, the idea prevailed that world champions would remain world champions in perpetuity. That was a fallacy, proven by Belgium's 5-1 watershed victory in Brussels. The Brazilians, however, weren't prepared yet to surrender their supremacy. They still felt spiritual masters of the game. The Europeans had come roaring back during that fateful tour in 1963, which signposted the demise of the Brazilian game. Friendly victories allowed Brazil to suppress a very uncomfortable truth a little longer. Actually, they should have rebuilt immediately after the 1962 World Cup.

Djalma Santos, Garrincha and Pelé were still world champions, even if they were in no state to play, even if they limped along on just one leg. So, what should have been a careful preparation for the 1966 World Cup descended into farce, with Moreira, and later Feola, showing a pathological faith in the veteran players. They didn't just fail in forcing the 1958–1962 generation to retire, but instead reinforced the myth of the invincible heroes.

The novices in the divided squad understood the gravitas of the situation but they were powerless to stand up to the veterans, whom they admired. Even the headstrong and inquisitive Gérson, whose injury prevented him from playing in Brazil's World Cup curtain-raiser against Bulgaria, was supine. He never contemplated insurrection. 'The older players yielded influence,' said Gérson. 'They came off the back of two World Cups. What were you going to say? We had no say.'

'We, the younger players, weren't allowed an opinion,' said Rildo. 'Dropping Carlos Alberto was the most ridiculous thing in the world, but who was I to run to the press and say that it was a terrible mistake? I was just a kid.'

There was very little accomplishment in defeating the Bulgarians, led by Rudolf Vytlačil, Czechoslovakia's 1962 World Cup coach. He tasked defensive destroyer Dobromir Zhechev to shadow Pelé. Zhechev's diligence in executing his duties wasn't very subtle. He endlessly pestered Pelé. In the 28th minute, the Brazilian retaliated. German referee Kurt Tschenscher and the other Brazilian players shielded Pelé from the aggrieved Bulgarians and the chutzpah of their feigned innocence.

The skirmish was fitting for an ill-tempered match. The Bulgarians littered play with malicious tackles but Brazil were fragmented, the players unfit and the football lukewarm. Strangely indolent, the South Americans never accelerated when necessary. They left too much space in between the lines and, when attacking, it was striking how often Brazil employed the long ball. At best, the 2-0 victory, the very last time Pelé and Garrincha played together in a series of 44 undefeated matches, was an agitated display from a superpower in complete disarray. 'It deceived the whole of Brazil into thinking they could win the World Cup,' said Rildo.

Brazil's illusions were falling away quickly. The win against Bulgaria revealed Brazil's limits, but the scope and scale of the crisis after the Hungary defeat were unprecedented. The match was an instant, indelible classic; the craft of the Hungarians exposed an opponent split along generational fault lines. Poignantly, the East Europeans had stuck to a small party. On the eve of the World Cup, the secretary of the Hungarian Football Federation, the Magyar Labdarúgó Szövetség, Gyorgi Honti, said, 'We find that the men who do not get a place in the side begin to nag. So, we cut down on the nagging by making the party as small as possible.'

Did Feola's team not possess a clear strategy then? At the 1966 World Cup, counter-attack was the best form of attack, at least that was the inference after the first matches, including the dire curtain-raiser between hosts England and Uruguay, but, in Group 3, Brazil, Bulgaria, Hungary and Portugal all defied the defensive trend. The Hungarians and the Portuguese quickly shed the safety-first tactics and illuminated the ten-day-long tedium of the first round. Hungary vs Brazil was, arguably, the best match of the tournament. It was a wondrous and dramatic encounter at Goodison Park, even without the injured Pelé.

The Magyars, once the masters of post-war football, married bold enterprise with sophistication, whereas the Brazilians played football at the speed of the 1962 World Cup with personnel of 1958. At an average age of 31, their backline represented a bygone era. Further upfield, the 32-year-old Garrincha played in his third finals. During the match he reached the byline only once, a dramatic and telling stat.

The Brazilians were bystanders, the veteran rearguard overcome by the velocity and flux of the opposing frontmen – wingers Ferenc Bene and Gyula Rákosi, centre-forwards János Farkas and Flórián Albert, whose intelligent runs opened up space for the midfielders and even for defenders Kálmán Mészöly and Ferenc Sipos, who was the Hungarian captain. The Europeans outnumbered Gérson and Lima in midfield.

In the 14th minute, Tostão cancelled out the audacious second-minute strike of Bene, who'd slalomed past Paulo Henrique, Altair and Bellini. The 1-1 half-time score didn't reflect the match's balance of power. The quicksilver Bene, deployed on the right, fooled Brazilian left-back Paulo Henrique. Raposzta's overlap was almost as menacing as Bene tucked inside and Flórián Albert's raids further confused Paulo Henrique. 'Albert didn't give you any time,' said Paulo Henrique, who played alongside Albert during the Hungarian's brief spell at Flamengo in 1968. 'He left our central defender Altair for dead to strike in the near corner; a great goal.'

It was Albert, the successor of the legendary Nándor Hidegkuti, who engineered Hungary's supremacy and thrilling win. A master tactician, he dictated the flow of his team's attack. With flawless dribbling and passing, he dropped deeper to draw Bellini away from the penalty area. Hungary swooped in and Brazil were quickly swept aside. It's almost an insult to only eulogise Albert without acknowledging the contributions of Bene and Farkas too. In a sequence of perfect motion and movement, these three standout stars combined for Hungary's second goal, a swirling volley from Farkas. Albert sent Bene striding down the right, where he jinxed away from a hapless Paulo Henrique to deliver a cross met with sinew-straining precision by Hungary's No. 10.

They were everything you imagined the Brazilians to be. They dreamed up a new football, whereas Brazil were hanging on to a game of the past. It was only Hungary's strange profligacy in front of goal, the cause of their opening 3-1 defeat by Portugal, that prevented a slaughter. 'We felt Pelé's absence,' said Paulo Henrique. 'I did. The opponent was afraid to man-mark him and you had Garrincha on the wing, who also invoked fear. They had studied Pelé, filmed him in Brazil, to find out how they were going to mark him.'

Even so, never had defending champions been on the brink of a first-round World Cup exit with so few good excuses. After the match, Brazil's directors refrained from talking to the international press. This time, they couldn't simply dismiss and downplay events. This was a major drama of Brazilian design.

Havelange's reaction to Brazil's first competitive defeat since the 1954 World Cup was not edifying. Irked by Bulgaria's violent play in the curtain-raiser, the Brazilian supremo and his deputy Nascimento wrote to FIFA, demanding that referees uphold fair-play norms. Before the Portugal match, Brazil's last group fixture, he complained to the world federation that the match referee and linesmen were English. In the knockout phase, referees should be assigned matches by lottery, he argued. His actions fuelled South American conspiracy theories over bias in favour of England. His public remonstrations were futile, yet perfect to cover up his own dereliction of duty. They distorted and misrepresented the reasons for Brazil's inglorious demise. In 1958 and 1962, Paulo Machado had engineered the Seleção's success, but Havelange's fleeting presence during Brazil's 1966 campaign didn't support his credentials and claims of being a performant administrator. He left the chaos unchecked.

On top of that, Havelange rolled out excuses. His classic blame-shifting stretched back as far as Brazil's 1954 World Cup quarter-final elimination, a match of great brutality against Hungary as well. Havelange's festering resentment was hypocritical. At a crucial juncture in the 1962 World Cup, Brazil benefited from 'refereeing bias' when Chilean referee Sergio Bustamante didn't award a penalty against Nilton Santos for bringing down Spain's Enrique Collar. Amarildo maintained that it was a correct decision. He said: 'Nilton committed the foul, the referee blew the whistle and he left his feet over the line. He had moved incredibly quickly, so the referee decided that the foul happened outside the box. He was very experienced, you know. Perhaps another player would have stayed in his original position.'

In England there was no reversing Brazil's disintegration. The team required a three-goal victory against Portugal to reach the quarter-finals. The sense of disarray and panic was so acute that Nascimento seized total control of the team. 'Feola didn't lead,' said Rildo. 'We felt that, in the team selection, in everything. Feola did the talking but, from the very start in Brazil, Nascimento picked the team. He led everything. He was the second in line after Havelange.'

It was a belated and clumsy attempt at rectifying the endless dithering over team selection. The supervisor maintained Lima and Jairzinho from the previous match, shifting the Botafogo player to the outside-left position. Pelé's return was a sign of desperation, even if convention tied Brazil's fate to his. He simply wasn't fit. Nascimento's course of action was, in truth, a final act of self-destruction. He fielded six players without any World Cup experience. Brazil were caught in a time warp, as if they were back in training in Lambari, endlessly tinkering with the first-team line-up but never quite settling on a formation.

Orlando had played in that first run-out in Lambari and now returned for Brazil's third group match. The 1958 veteran was no match for Portuguese star player Eusébio's great feline strength and skills. Before the half-hour mark, both he and Simões scored. The Portuguese often, however, had little interest in connecting with the ball. With great insistence, João Morais and Vicente, his old rival, hacked relentlessly at Pelé. There was something cold, calculating and cynical about the Portuguese's dispassionate brutality, in complete contrast with the periods when they played with beauty and grace. Yet the provocations and violence from Vicente and his henchmen directed at a team on its knees didn't move English referee George McCabe. 'He didn't protect Pelé or anyone else,' complained Rildo, although he largely refrained from invoking the Portuguese's roughness as an excuse.

Football in the 1960s was simply hard, and in the 31st minute Morais targeted Pelé one time too many. José Augusto denied that Otto Glória, Portugal's Brazilian coach, had instructed his players to foul Pelé deliberately, but the outcome was all the same; Brazil's talisman was crippled and his team broken. 'The Portuguese meant to destroy the match and they succeeded,' said Batuta, who, in his only ever World Cup match, replaced Tostão. 'The fans were also frustrated because Pelé could no longer deliver the gift that God had given him, his art.'

'Pelé was the saviour of the fatherland, yes, but he needed help,' said Denilson.

'When Pelé got hurt, our confidence sank,' said Batuta, who got injured as well after a collision with Costa Pereira, Portugal's experienced goalkeeper. 'It killed the match.' The players' morale dropped. By half-time, they needed five goals. In the stands, Paulo Henrique was yelling in disbelief at the impotence and apathy of his team-mates. The undertaking was Herculean or, in Rildo's view, 'truly, humanly impossible'.

With grim inevitability, the match wound to its logical conclusion. On the left wing, Pelé was now a spectator. The intensity of the peevish Portuguese dropped. They no longer hurried and harried midfield halves Lima and Denilson, but allowed Brazil possession. The Portuguese were cynical, yet not sadistic; they didn't want to humiliate Brazil.

In a rare moment of attacking creativity midway through the second half, Rildo, with the élan of his predecessor Nilton Santos, burst forward and combined with Jairzinho to cut Portugal's advantage. Brazil, however, were ghosts of their former selves. 'Portugal could have won by six,' said Jairzinho. 'That's how disorganised Brazil were.'

Fittingly, it was Eusébio's 85th-minute goal that deposed the fading champions. His strike, a half-volley hit with all the thunder his potent right foot could summon, was ruthless; his skill needed no embellishment.

Eusébio, the European player of the year, assumed Pelé's mantle as the best player in the world. The Portuguese team remained unassailable until McCabe's final whistle. 'It was an XI in the first game, and another XI in the second and a different XI in the third game,' said Gérson. 'It was no use.'

In the dressing room, amid a sea of tears, a scolding from either Feola, Nascimento or Havelange, depending on different versions of events, did little to palliate the crushing finality of defeat. 'It was like a family member had died,' said Denilson.

Some of Brazil's players had long passed their natural points of no return. Stars die in different ways. Some balloon up into red giants in one final blaze of glory and then shrink into a shadow of their former selves. Others simply go dark. The Seleção imploded and fizzled out, bringing their brilliant existence to a violent, dramatic conclusion. Brazil's defenestration, at the hands of Flórián Albert and Eusébio, was humiliating and profoundly sad.

This was a final goodbye to Garrincha, a final goodbye to Gilmar and other luminaries. The eight-day disaster in England proved how fragile they'd become. At Goodison Park, their unforgettable beauty was fading. Their triumphs were as spectacular as their defeats. Since those extraordinary three minutes in 1958 against the USSR, their football had seemed a miracle, their game a balm to the soul. After the 1962 World Cup in Chile, Brazil, however, had turned inwards, something Otto Glória pointed out. He said, 'The game that Brazil gave to the world has been overtaken. The Brazilians – obsessed by their successes of 1958 and 1962 – couldn't see that.' The Brazilians had forgotten that football ultimately is dialectical. New styles and shapes counter the philosophy of the dominant team. It's a process that's endlessly repeated.

In England, Brazil were the team everyone had yearned to beat, so, in response to their hegemony, European teams crowded the midfield, playing more compact, multifunctional and physical football, something Gérson called '*futebol força*'. Brazil's tactics were rendered obsolete. They played with fixed wingers who contributed little to defence. On the left, Jairzinho was cut hopelessly adrift. On the right, Garrincha simply didn't have the physique to track back. Brazil had regressed to a 4-2-4.

'I cried on the trip back, I cried on arrival in Rio, I cried at home,' remembered Paulo Henrique. 'I had prepared to be a world champion. I simply cried for two months.'

Pensive, Denilson shrugged at the entire memory. He couldn't explain why and how Brazil exited the 1966 World Cup and struggled to reconcile himself with the scale of the disaster. Poignantly, he blamed everyone and no one. Failure is a collective responsibility, he argued, refusing to accept the harsher reality that Brazil's preparation shaped a team that was destined to fail.

Outspoken, Rildo's words were often laced with dark disillusionment about the puppet-master powers that were and how their covert machinations destroyed what could have been the pinnacle of his individual career. In his view, the CBD, like in 1963, exploited the Seleção.

Lima lamented the excesses of 1966. Everything, to his mind, was exaggerated: the practices, the parades and all the players involved. 'There was too much optimism,' said Lima. 'Many people thought that Brazil had already won the third world title. This perhaps infected our group.'

'The group of players were older than the game allows,' added Paulo Henrique.

Brazil's elimination marked the end of a generation and shattered Rodrigues's and Havelange's shared image of Brazilian exceptionalism. They ignored the complex historical process behind Brazil's rise and fall; the invention of the back four and the meticulous preparation in 1958 with an expanded backroom staff.

Brazil could no longer detach themselves from reality, but perhaps there was a silver lining to their premature exit: it needn't be the end of an era yet. The disposed champions still had magnificent and almost unparalleled resources with the raw talent of Carlos Alberto, Brito, Gérson, Jairzinho and Tostão. At 25, Pelé's prime was theoretically still in front of him.

The crisis demanded a response that was swift, rational and collective. How could Brazil win the World Cup again? Hiking in the mountains of Rio de Janeiro, Lamartine DaCosta, who had no particular liking for football, would provide a part of the answer.

Chapter IV

The Technocrats

IN THE 1950s and 1960s, playwright Nelson Rodrigues's evocative writing manipulated Brazil's national psyche, knitting together a narrative of a country in football boots, with players simply outscoring the opponent and dancing to victory in a joyous interpretation of the game. It's a line of thinking that still survives, entangled in myth and specious ideas, perpetuated by the Brazilian football establishment and ultimately exacerbated by the international press.

This fantasy dominated the Brazilian game in the late 1960s, even if results had proven that improvisation was no longer enough to win. The 1963 humiliation against Belgium was widely seen as an aberration but the disastrous elimination in the group stages of the 1966 World Cup demonstrated that Brazilian football needed reappraisal.

The European teams had been physically superior. Hence, the Brazilians, too, needed to be fit. Army commander Lamartine DaCosta subscribed to this view. Brazilian athletes struggled in adverse conditions and football players' levels of intensity often dropped in the second half. Brazilians lacked stamina – a significant concern before the 1970 World Cup in Mexico, where altitude and heat would require peak physical fitness.

It was a point he tried to get across to João Saldanha, Brazil's head coach. In the autumn of 1969, accompanied by captain Claudio Coutinho, they met in Churrascaria Urca, a famous BBQ restaurant at the foot of Pão de Açúcar, Rio's Sugarloaf Mountain. The coach and the commander sized each other up. Saldanha carried himself with the nonchalance of a bohemian. He wasn't unpleasantly self-conscious but, at times, seemed agitated in conversation. The Brazil coach was as civil as he was cultivated, a bit sceptical, sometimes scoffing, but never vulgar. Saldanha wasn't particularly fond of the military; his own Marxist beliefs opposed the views of the ruling junta.

For all intents and purposes, DaCosta wasn't just any commander either. A specialist in biometeorology, an interdisciplinary science that examines the interactions between atmospheric phenomena and living organisms, he taught at the Pontifícia Universidade Católica do Rio de Janeiro. He had little love for Brazil's favourite pastime and likened football players to children; in his opinion, they had few, if any, intellectual faculties. At a coffee bar in Leblon in 2019, DaCosta asked me, 'What will you do with children?' … and he chuckled.

All these many years later, his view of Brazilian football and its flaws hadn't changed much. 'There was a cultural belief that the Brazilian player was superior,' said DaCosta. 'You couldn't and can't deal with people who believe things are mythological. All Brazilian clubs did the same things more or less; exercises, running and weights, but the physical preparation was hardly scientific. Results need to be quantified. The 1970 World Cup in Mexico was good in that way. It pressed Saldanha and the Brazilians: "adapt or lose".'

DaCosta's message for Saldanha, delivered on that autumn afternoon in 1969, was irreconcilable with much of what Brazilian football had stood for. It was imperative that Saldanha understood its significance. Instead, he just frowned and took a swig of his beer.

* * *

Rio de Janeiro's military school of physical education, the Escola de Educação Física do Exército (EsEFEx), is hidden in plain sight, at the tip of a headland that juts into Guanabara bay. From the top of Sugarloaf Mountain, you can see the military base's football pitch, athletics track, tennis courts and even the secluded beach volleyball courts. Founded in 1922, the school was built to promote physical education for both the military and civilians and provide them with state-of-the-art facilities. On its corrugated roof, the words '*Exército Brasileiro*' (Brazilian Army) sit painted in bright, white letters. In the distance, a part of the outer wall of the São José Fort is just visible, revealing the historical significance of the site. The Fort is the military base where, on 1 March 1565, the Portuguese first settled. Adjacent to the school's football pitch, a bronze, commemorative plaque honours Estácio de Sá, the founder of Rio de Janeiro.

Today, Sugarloaf Mountain is the star attraction of the Urca neighbourhood, a little village on its own. Urca is clustered at the foot of the hill, populated by the middle class and strewn with houses in Art Deco, Manuelino and mock-Tudor style. The tourists at Bar Urca, iconic for serving ice-cold beer and fried snacks at the dreamy waterfront, will hardly notice the entrance to the military school at the end of the winding road.

It was through that gate, in the 1950s, that DaCosta walked to pursue a military education. Yet he had no interest in devoting a lifetime of service to the army. To nurture an interest in sports and escape from the navy, he enrolled in the military pentathlon, a sport based on the modern pentathlon but adapted to the needs of the army. A French major had pioneered the discipline after watching Dutch army parachutists dropping over land to cover a 20km obstacle course.

With great interest, DaCosta watched Brazilian soldiers practise and perfect their skills in this novel sport. They shot their rifles with precision and speed, manoeuvred their way past tripwires, swam past even more obstacles and threw inactive grenades at distances of up to 35 metres. The shooting, obstacle course, swimming, throwing and cross-country were all disciplines that demanded great physical fitness.

The sport was growing and the Brazilian team won a maiden world title on home soil in 1960. Soldier Barnabé Santos was Brazil's undisputed star, excelling at the Vasco da Gama swimming pool, the shooting range of the Vila Militar and the other competitions in Urca.

'He was a sensational athlete,' recalled Orlando Cani, a parachute sergeant who competed in the military pentathlon for Brazil from 1958 to 1965. 'And a very quick learner. Barnabé had the perfect height, about 1m 78cm or 1m 80cm, for the obstacle run. He had great motor skills as well and was invincible in swimming. He owned that discipline.'

On the track of the military school, Santos and Brazil dominated the obstacle run; 500m with 20 standardised obstacles, including a rope ladder, double beam and a tripwire. Santos clocked a winning time of 2:33.8, with captain Nilo da Silva coming in as runner-up in 2:35.2. At the end of the day's competition, French sergeant Mohamed Sahli reflected, 'What surprises me the most is the physical condition of the Brazilian athletes. This discipline is traditionally dominated by the French and the Swedes.'

Perhaps Brazilians were becoming more mature competitors in the military pentathlon. DaCosta felt differently, however; Brazil's dominance in 1960 sprang from their home advantage. In his view, Brazil's athletes weren't any good at competing on foreign soil. And, Santos was no different in that regard: he mostly won in 'tropical' Brazil.

Initially, DaCosta attributed the underwhelming results of Brazilian athletes to a tendency for superstition when out of their comfort zone or a sense of inferiority that pervaded their minds when abroad. He wondered why the results in the 8km cross-country race had been particularly disappointing. 'Brazil was not good at running, and that was a problem,' admitted Cani, who today runs a yoga institute in Copacabana. 'In relation to the Europeans and Scandinavians, we were weak in cross-country. There was little tradition. It was definitely not our greatest asset.'

DaCosta conducted a study over the same distance in Barra da Tijuca, a stretch of marshland in Rio, that revealed a considerable drop in athletic performance. He reasoned that either the training methods or the environment were responsible. In Brazil, interval training, alternating short bursts of intense activity with longer intervals of relief periods or rest, replaced the arduous monotony of continuous training in the

1960s. It became a dominant training method for both swimmers and runners, strengthening their cardiovascular fitness and speed. Enthused, Cani experimented with interval training, shaving his time in the obstacle run by three seconds, down from two minutes 50 seconds. Interval training, then, was clearly not a negative factor.

When not analysing the military pentathlon, DaCosta enjoyed hiking in the Serra dos Órgãos, a mountain range just north of Rio de Janeiro blanketed by indigenous forests and vegetation. As he explored heights above 670m, DaCosta felt the sun's impact. His skin crisped and his eyes itched. His throat was dry and his lungs were gasping for more oxygen. The existing literature in biometeorology detailed these discomforts. He realised that solar radiation had an impact at altitude as well.

To explore the effect, DaCosta wanted the pentathletes to abandon the track or the beach, conventional training spots that offered little or no protection against the sun. Athletes from Rio de Janeiro and the Brazilian hinterland were often subjected to a brutal tropical environment. In summer, Rio's humidity skyrocketed to 90 per cent and the heat peaked, affecting an athlete's resistance and endurance. In such conditions, it was impossible to achieve sporting excellence. Cani, a *Carioca*, remarked apropos the high temperatures: 'I trained for the military pentathlon sometimes in 35°, 38° or 40°C. Totally exhausting!'

DaCosta chose a new training location: the Floresta da Tijuca, the dense national park within the confines of the city with an elevation up to 900m, and housed Santos, Ulisses and six other athletes at the nearby Maracanã. The forest's canopy protected the athletes from the oppressive sun, resulting in a temperature drop of 5° to 6°C. It seemed he'd found the right climate conditions.

It was impossible not to notice something peculiar was going on: his skilled and experienced athletes recorded times that oscillated wildly. They ran in slow motion as if held back by an invisible force. The forest's coolness seemed irrelevant; athletic performances nosedived. To his frustration, DaCosta couldn't quite pinpoint how and why altitude slowed down his athletes. He wasn't alone. In the 1960s, altitude frustrated and confounded all of those who looked into it. The phenomenon induced worldwide fascination.

* * *

In October 1968, Mexico City was staging the Olympic Games, a unique opportunity for the hosts to reframe Mexico's global reputation. They wanted to banish Latin stereotypes. 'Mexico was in a difficult economic moment, but there were some mean and nasty questions from journalists: "Do you have milk?"' remembered

Felipe Muñoz, Mexico's youngest-ever gold medallist, who, at the age of 17, claimed the 200m breaststroke. 'They thought we slept in hammocks.'

The Games were to be 'swifter, stronger and higher' than any other. The altitude claim was uncontested. At 2,240m, the Mexican capital rests on a lake bed situated on a plateau, surrounded by mountains. At the time, no major international sporting event had ever been staged as high above sea level. Altitude rattled the entire equation of fair competition. Mexico's bid book tried to reassure everyone: a few days of acclimatisation would suffice for active athletes to compete in Mexico City; athletes living at altitude wouldn't benefit from any advantage. IOC president Avery Brundage backed Mexico, defending the universality of the Games. He said: 'The Olympic Games belong to the entire world, not just to the part at sea level.'

But the questions simply wouldn't go away: how could athletes at sea level acclimatise to altitude without preventing a loss in performance? Were wealthier nations, with more resources at their disposal, at an advantage? Did altitude increase rather than narrow inequality and exclusion? Did the IOC think of extending the maximum training time for athletes and thus revise its strict definition of amateurism?

To address the mounting pressure, Mexico staged pre-Olympic weeks in 1965 and 1966 to simulate Olympic conditions for research purposes. Suddenly, altitude physiology and a detailed study of oxygen uptake, the respiratory system, the blood and the cardiovascular system were fashionable once more. Scientific interest in thin air was piqued. The subject had largely lain dormant after the first boom in alpinism and the quest to scale Mount Everest drove the first wave of academic studies in the 19th and early 20th centuries. The Second World War and the continued development of fighter jets then prompted further research. However, alpinism and aviation were strictly high-altitude endeavours. They had little to do with sports at medium altitude, between 1,800m and 3,000m. At both the 1926 Central American Games and the 1955 Pan-American Games in the Mexican capital, altitude was a concern so inconsequential that it was mostly ignored.

The 1965 and 1966 athletic meets in Mexico City were a curiosity, with Romanian rowers, British runners and Belgian athletes among the guinea pigs, completing endless questionnaires, donating blood and competing in custom-built suits and special masks. Trackside, a battery of doctors and academics chased the athletes down for testing.

Acclaimed American long-distance runner Billy Mills wrote, 'There is the awful sensation of breathing deeply and not being able to pull enough air into your lungs. When you run, you feel like you've never run before.' With his speed, strength and coordination still intact, Mill's resistance and endurance evaporated. A consensus existed that altitude sapped performance because of hypoxia, but the training time required to counter the oxygen debt and adapt to altitude was contentious.

Both the French and Germans suggested three weeks of acclimatisation for the Olympic Games in Mexico but they disagreed on the necessary duration of a preceding altitude camp in the Alps; the Belgians proposed two weeks at altitude in Europe followed by two weeks in Mexico. The Spanish differentiated according to the sport. Renowned physiologist Dr Griffith Pugh and the English claimed four weeks would suffice.

The hosts maximised home advantage. Muñoz, a native of Mexico City, had trained for weeks, months and years at the state-of-the-art Olympic Sports Centre. Every day he swam up to 15 kilometres to develop his body and aerobic capacity. 'My American coach Ron Johnson said: "You Mexicans have that advantage over everybody,"' said Muñoz. 'Every time we swam at sea level we performed better and returning to Mexico City it took time to catch up again.'

The growing clamour and confusion over altitude didn't disconcert DaCosta. He didn't object to Mexico staging the Games, neither did he ever profess an impending disaster for the competing athletes. In 1967 the Brazilian government tasked him to explore the climate conditions on site and map out a meticulous plan for the Olympic delegation. That's when local cardiologists whispered in his ear, 'Go and have a look at Guanajuato.'

A 350-kilometre drive north-east of the Mexican capital, he discovered a colourful, provincial city with cobbled streets that married both the desired altitude and climate with acceptable facilities. The city had built itself a certain renown for curing the ill, he was told. While there, DaCosta also noticed that the sun beat down even harder than in Rio's national park.

Based on his experience with the military pentathlon, the battery of academic studies at his disposal and his own visit to Mexico, he wrote *Planejamento Mexico*, a comprehensive guide for Brazil's Olympic delegation to navigate the climate and altitude in the Mexican capital. The handbook detailed how swimmers were most prone to diarrhoea, basketball players' and fencers' arms would tire faster and, as DaCosta pointed out, athletic performances would suffer in all aerobic events as a result of the drop in oxygen level. With an acute understanding that any knowledge about the cellular dynamics of the human body at altitude was incomplete, DaCosta, as a solution, suggested gradual acclimatisation over three to five weeks, first at home, then in Mexico.

Before departure to Mexico City, he proposed an altitude camp at 1,600m in Campos do Jordão in São

Paulo's mountains. Brazil's rugged relief extends along the coast and penetrates the interior near the centres of urban development, notably in Rio de Janeiro, São Paulo, Minas Gerais, Santa Catarina and Paraná. These regions offer unique microclimates, like Teresopolis.

The Olympic football team, all amateurs, spent a couple of weeks in Campos do Jordão before embarking for Mexico. In the final round of Olympic qualifiers, Brazil saw off Colombia, Uruguay and Paraguay in Bogotá, at an altitude of 2,640m. They then arrived in good shape in the Olympic village. 'The camp in Campos do Jordão was to adapt to altitude,' recalled centre-forward Manoel Maria, who also featured alongside Pelé at Santos. 'I came from Para, the north of Brazil, so it was a cold city. In Colombia there was a bit of altitude as well, but I neither drank nor smoked so my physical condition was good. In Mexico none of us were affected. We got on with it.'

Even so, Brazil's Olympic adventure was short-lived. Maria got sent off in a 1-0 defeat against Spain in Mexico City and, following the injury of forward China, the team's attacking prowess was diminished, resulting in draws with both Japan and Nigeria in Puebla, and, ultimately, early elimination. In an all-Eastern European final, Hungary won the gold medal 4-1 against Bulgaria.

In FIFA's technical study, previewing the 1970 World Cup, Dettmar Cramer wrote that 'top form must be reached prior to arrival', that 'the teams should arrive in Mexico three to four weeks before the first match', and that 'it is advisable to stay and to practise at the altitude of Toluca, i.e. 2,700m above sea level. In this way, the acclimatisation difficulties at the lower level of the other places will be easier to overcome.'

Although the football team might have accepted DaCosta's theory on oxygen debt, the majority of Brazil's Olympic delegation weren't impressed. Coaches largely dismissed the idea of gradual acclimatisation, he recalled.

As medal candidates, Brazil's basketball team was one of the last members of the delegation to arrive in the Mexican capital in October, just 11 days before tip-off. They'd trained for weeks in Rio de Janeiro. There was little concern over altitude. The team automatically combined technique, tactics and physical conditioning during training, melding these skills together on the court. Coach Renato Cunha led practice and a masseur was on standby. 'Train, train, run, run, throw, throw and play,' recalled star player Wlamir Marques, who in daily life worked at the post office. 'We didn't even have a physiotherapist.' Marques had played in Mexico before. The altitude and rarefied air were a concern for him. The players were submitted to tests in a hypobaric chamber, which simulated an altitude of up to 5,000m. The doctor on site said that the team would be acclimatised five days after arrival in Mexico.

'You run, move and don't stop in basketball,' said Marques, whose team finished fourth in the end. 'It is a sport of constant attack and defence. You tire. A basketball player would feel the atmospheric pressure more than a football player. You felt it, the lack of air. You didn't train normally in the first few days but, for a competition of 10 to 15 days, we arrived in advance and had time to adapt. Besides, altitude is an individual problem. I played in Quito and, on the bench, you had oxygen masks. You played for five, six, seven minutes, left the court and took a breath of oxygen.'

In the pool, José Fiolo, the country's main medal aspirant, arrived in Mexico on the first day of October, 18 days before the 100m breaststroke event. His potential and talent were undisputed. Aged 17, he'd broken the world record with a time of 1:06.4. On arrival, Fiolo got sick, complaining of muscle aches, which truncated his training schedule. By the time his competitors were swimming ten kilometres a day, he was still adapting to the climate and taking on just about half of the workload, much to the chagrin of his coach Roberto Pavel. To distract himself, Fiolo read Hermann Hesse's novel, *Siddhartha*.

As the lure of Olympic glory wasn't always enough for Fiolo to train with the discipline that elite swimming demanded, Pavel sent him to Cani for training that focused on his respiration. To little avail. At Botafogo, where Fiolo trained, the pool was semi-covered, the water wavy and the temperatures cold in July and August, the winter months in Rio de Janeiro. 'It was darn hard to spend hours in that kind of water,' reflected Fiolo on a call from Australia, his adopted home. 'The outside temperature does not reflect the temperature inside a non-heated pool. The water's temperature drops at least 5°C. Botafogo's pool was the coldest in town!'

The issue of non-heated pools also explained why Fiolo didn't opt for gradual acclimatisation at altitude in Brazil. 'There was no point in finding a higher training venue because we didn't have heated pools,' said Fiolo. 'The higher you go, the colder it's gonna get.'

After two weeks of training at various Mexican clubs, Fiolo entered the 100m breaststroke final as one of the favourites. Explosive and fast, he shed the strategy of a negative split, but in the last 30 metres, his pedigree failed him. His muscles and entire body tensed up. Struggling, he swam the last metres almost beneath the lane rope. The Brazilian missed the podium by one-hundredth of a second.

On the sidelines, DaCosta remained a keen observer. When not indulging himself a little at the local nightclub, or smoking a little pot with captain Coutinho, the assistant volleyball coach, he watched competitions, Fiolo in the pool and Marques on the court.

With three medals, Brazil emulated the achieve-ments of their best-ever results, the 1952 Helsinki

Games and the 1920 Antwerp Games. Brazil's silver medallist long jumper Nelson Prudencio was a victim of Bob Beamon's incredible feat. The American didn't simply surpass the world record but shattered it. His generational jump incorporated skill, technique, fitness and perhaps even benefited from the thin air.

* * *

Back at the Churrascaria, Saldanha was still suspicious of DaCosta, this technocrat, this man with military schooling. Yet it was DaCosta and other coaches who updated and modernised training methods. Clipboard in hand, they followed and monitored the progress of their charges. Everything was measured and calculated. It wasn't just about accumulating data and quantification; they pioneered a different approach to sports. They wanted to manage the field through science. Military pentathlon, swimming, athletics and football all served as a laboratory for understanding and improving athletic performance.

The technocrats' presence in sports and football went hand in hand with the proliferation of their brethren in all spheres of Brazilian society. They laid the groundwork for a new model of government and unfettered capitalism in Brazil. In 1964, the junta leader, General Castelo Branco, delegated power over economic and fiscal policies to the technocrats. Elected by no one and faceless, they were the planners, economists, engineers and technicians who really ran Brazil. They were at liberty to experiment but remained 'politically neutral'. They modernised the state apparatus and attracted foreign capital but never risked altering social equilibriums. Slowly, a new Brazil was taking shape, formed by a regime that was at once bureaucratic and authoritarian. This new nation was buttressed by an alliance between the military, the burgeoning technocrats and the old elite.

In 1968, the military introduced the AI-5, the notorious Institutional Act Number Five, which heralded hard-line rule, beckoning the darkest years of the dictatorship. It was the legal framework that allowed for an arbitrary clampdown on civil society. In the cabinet of President Costa e Silva, and under the rule of General Emílio Garrastazu Médici, technocrats were ubiquitous. An economics professor from São Paulo, Antonio Delfim Neto, the minister of planning, was chief among them, often credited with instigating the 'Brazilian miracle'.

DaCosta, who shied away from politics, said:

'I confess. I belong to that technocratic generation, but it was behaviour that I was imbued with. Coutinho and I came out of the technocratic field and influenced the Seleção. Any analysis of the 1970 World Cup must be that it was profoundly technocratic ... Technocracy dominated. We were the China of the 1960s and the 1970s. In various years, the growth was 11 per cent. Those were the first steps into the future. The government was interested in building highways and power plants. Itaipu was home to the world's largest dam. In the field of physical education, the elite was also educated and financed by the military government. The dictatorship took on the mess that the country was, but a myth was created that everything worked and that we were living a dream. It was unreasonable and an illusion. On the one hand, the economy was booming and on the other hand, the people were doing very badly, right?'

DaCosta also pointed out that 'Out of 1.2 million applicants for the army, 80 per cent were dismissed because they had neither the weight nor the height and were full of diseases. The numbers said that in Brazil sports couldn't be practised the way it was done in Europe.' For a population that was poor and thus largely unfit, the feats of sporting greatness achieved by tennis star Maria Esther Bueno and a few others were exceptional.

Physical preparation was basic. Cani and Marques complained about the need for more coaches. Fiolo's fitness regime was very elementary. He exercised with a few dumbbells and weights at home. Brazilian football clubs often employed physical coaches, who maintained their players' fitness with very simple exercises. Lima remembered running near Santos's pristine seafront as part of the club's fitness routine.

Gérson recalled a typical exercise of the time at Flamengo under Fleitas Solich. He said, 'Run, jump over obstacles, jump to head a ball and a metre or two later you would receive a ball to shoot at goal.'

Tostão's experience at Cruzeiro was comparable. He recalled, 'Training was the *coletivo*, 90 minutes as if it were a game. The next day, you ran up and down the stairs or clapped your hands. I am not joking.'

The arrival of physical coach Julio Mazzei in 1964 benefited Santos's players greatly and allowed the team to maintain their gruelling but lucrative international touring schedule.

Mazzei had pursued a postgraduate in sports education from the University of Michigan. In his autobiography, Pelé pointed out that 'he presented a far different picture from most of the trainers in Brazilian clubs at the time'.

Mazzei introduced both interval and circuit training at the Vila Belmiro. He nurtured strong relationships with the players to understand their individual biology and needs. Midfielders needed endurance, full-backs and outside-forwards required speed, while inside-forwards and defenders yearned for agility. 'He would ask: "What do you need?"' explained Lima. 'That was unheard of. You'd reply: "Professor, I had these difficulties and was struggling from the 40th minute in the second half." So, he adapted your workload.'

A superb winger, Edu concurred: 'He gave the opportunity for dialogue. I did short sprints instead of running up and down the stairs.'

At Botafogo, Admildo Chirol, a graduate from the Universidade Federal do Estado do Rio de Janeiro, with its campus in Urca as well, modernised the team's physical conditioning. At his previous club, America, he'd moved away from simple military-inspired callisthenics to introduce assessments of both the players' cardiorespiratory fitness and muscle strength. In his view, physical fitness required more than simply mimicking matches in training.

Midfielder Afonsinho arrived at Botafogo in 1965 as a frail teenager from the interior, but Chirol transformed him into an athlete. Later, when Afonsinho became alienated from the club following a dispute with coach Mário Zagallo, Chirol handed him an individual programme based on circuit training. 'I really struggled with the introduction and the evolution of physical preparation,' said Afonsinho. 'Chirol was very in tune with things. He introduced working with different loads and training at the actual kick-off time of the matches, *em tempo integral.*'

Even so, DaCosta, Mazzei and Chirol all venerated the technocratic ideal. In a quick-burst revolution, they shifted the emphasis in Brazilian football from technique to physical preparation. Coutinho and Carlos Alberto Parreira, an EsEFEx alumnus with military qualifications as well, were also proponents of the same school of thought. But 'Brazil has never got rid of the ideas which were implanted at the time,' lamented Afonsinho.

Saldanha knew of the need for a better physical preparation. As a columnist for *A Ultima Hora*, he'd witnessed Brazil's 1966 debacle first-hand. What he'd seen from the Europeans had frightened him. He summed up the opening match between hosts England and Uruguay as 'a mix of basketball, rugby and horse racing' and decried 'the boxing scene produced by the mean Stiles'. That's why, although reluctantly, he'd tried to contact DaCosta. But the commander was nowhere to be found. The Brazil coach wondered whether this expert wasn't fictitious.

However, at last, DaCosta returned his call: 'Is Mr Saldanha still searching for me? Now, a little detail: I am not a colonel. I am from the navy and I am not called Lamarino, all right? My name is Lamartine, commander Lamartine. What can I help you with?'

They decided to meet and, as the afternoon progressed in Urca, the alcohol was beginning to have its effect on Saldanha. Slightly drunk and restless, he was of the opinion that DaCosta was perhaps another postulant who wanted to join the backroom staff of the Seleção. In truth, football was anathema to DaCosta, his antipathy stemming from his belief that football's environment was unprofessional. These revelations puzzled Saldanha as much as they intrigued him. Aloof, Coutinho mediated and Saldanha's apprehension turned into mild appreciation for DaCosta. Brazil's coach was prepared to hear him out.

DaCosta's pitch was simple: he wanted to introduce altitude training and turn football players into athletes. The 1968 Olympic Games were a useful portent to the 1970 World Cup, he believed. Altitude training was imperative for any chance of success. DaCosta drew a timeline on a napkin with a pencil to illustrate his point. The impromptu sketch resembled the higgledy-piggledy drawing of a five-year-old but contained the outline for Brazil's schedule leading to and during the World Cup. Players were to report for medical checks and physical aptitude tests. The training camp would commence in early February of 1970 with five weeks of basic conditioning at sea level in Rio de Janeiro, followed by a week of travel via Brasilia, Manaus and Bogotá to Mexico, and adaptation to altitude from the ninth to 12th week in Guadalajara at 1,680m above sea level. To achieve absolute peak physical fitness, acclimatisation would be gradual; after the first weeks in Guadalajara, Brazil would move to Guanajuato, at 2,050m, during the tournament itself. Full acclimatisation would be attained if Brazil reached the final in Mexico City, at 2,240m.

Saldanha was impressed by the sprawling galaxy of facts and data that DaCosta presented. The bottom line of his scientific thesis was crystalline: the game's significance was bestowed upon it by its heroes, but what good would the skill set of Pelé, Tostão and others be without any physical fitness? At altitude, they'd simply be paralysed.

'Saldanha is the hero of the story,' reflected DaCosta half a decade later. 'He discarded the myth. He was receptive and had the vision to organise the game, even if Brazilian football completely lacked a scientific climate. You could deduce that from his writings and TV appearances as well. Informed and experienced, he worried about the physical preparation.'

Unquestionably, Saldanha was a cultural icon of his time but, like every hero, he was flawed. In the summer of 1969, Brazil's head coach self-destructed, or did he?

Chapter V

The Dreamer

JOÃO HAVELANGE despaired. The Seleção was in perpetual crisis. The next global finals were on the horizon but, at the start of 1969, he was running a stagnant team. Brazil's popularity was plummeting rapidly. They were carrying the burden of success, and failure was no longer acceptable. The next World Cup had to be won.

Brazil's football boss needed a coach who could prove that the chaos and complacency of the 1966 World Cup hadn't yet destroyed Brazil's reputation. He wondered who could bring new impetus, rebuild the team, navigate the World Cup qualifiers and, above all, satisfy the fans?

Enter João Saldanha, a gloriously authentic personality, whose reign was a wonderful spectacle. Saldanha was a bohemian, communist, coach, journalist and dialectician. His mere presence incited intrigue, political plotting and subterfuge from the CBD, the press and the military, perhaps all the way up to the highest office, that of President Médici. His successes matched his failures and his virtues his flaws. His spats, feuds, cliques, rivalries and total disregard for the political hierarchy led to his own fall.

One can portray Saldanha but one can't understand him. Books, interviews and archives touch upon a modicum of the truth but never reveal who Saldanha really was. His personality and tenure with the national team remain shrouded in mystery, even to those who were closest to him.

Tostão summed it up: 'I adored him as a person. He was emotional and a humanist. He was a dreamer. He was the total opposite of what the establishment wanted of a coach but, on the other hand, he was popular. The CBD and the government wanted to charm. In truth, it was something half schizophrenic, with various sides [to the story], opaque and contradictory. You simply can't make a logical, correct analysis of his downfall.'

* * *

João Alves Jobim Saldanha was born on 3 July 1917, third son to Gaspar and Jenny Jobim Saldanha, in the village of Alegrete, Rio Grande do Sul, where he spent a formative part of his childhood imbued in the political agitation that so marked the state in the 19th and early 20th century.

The Saldanha family, rich farmers, were *Maragatos*, federalists who wanted independence for Brazil's southern states. They opposed the long reign of governor Augusto Borges de Medeiros, a *Chimango*, who enjoyed the support of the central government. In 1923 tensions between the fractions morphed into a Gaucho civil war, with the family actively engaging in guerrilla tactics. João and his older siblings, Aristides and Maria, smuggled arms and ammunition under their clothes. On the playground, the brothers re-enacted the war with their sister. They shouted: 'How do you want to die? By stabbing or by gunfire?'

The *Chimangos* prevailed and Gaspar Saldanha fled with his family to Uruguay before returning to Paraná. In 1928 he realigned his political views to support another *Chimango*, Getúlio Vargas. His loyalty was rewarded with financial security in the shape of a real estate office in Rio de Janeiro's wealthy Zona Sul, the south zone. The Saldanhas, once again, moved, and arrived in Brazil's capital and economic heartbeat in 1931.

Although as an adolescent João Saldanha was impressionable, the sensual grandeur of Rio de Janeiro couldn't entirely offset the importance of his childhood in shaping his character and personality. 'My father was from 1917, from the south, from an elite family,' said his son João Vitto Saldanha, a choreographer in Rio de Janeiro. 'That was his background. Farming.

His thinking was rural. He became refined over the years in Rio de Janeiro – his urban side – but in essence he was a man from the fields, from the farm, from Rio Grande do Sul, from Uruguay. His grandmother was very catholic. He questioned religion, but you can't simply break with that conservatism.'

His rural upbringing and the values it imparted clashed with the sophistication of the city and the world that lay beyond. Incontrovertibly, Rio de Janeiro transformed and politicised Saldanha, but never emasculated him. The core of his self-image was grounded in Rio Grande do Sul. In his son's view 'that thing from the hinterland' never left him.

In 1942, Saldanha, alongside his brother Aristides, became a member of the Partido Comunista Brasileiro (PCB), a party that had sprung from the anarchist movement, but remained mostly fractured and marginalised in Brazilian politics, drifting in and out of legality. Even so, it was the dominant force on the left.

The Saldanha brothers broke away from their father's centrist and liberal convictions. 'João and Aristides wanted to contribute to society by involvement in an organisation that was an enemy of the dominant class,' said Regis Frati, who joined the PCB in 1968 and met Saldanha for the first time in 1977. 'It wasn't just about fighting inequality, but doing so in the most radical way possible.'

An alderman in Rio de Janeiro for the Partido Republicano Trabalhista, Aristides was a prominent party member, whose commanding eloquence, intelligence and loyalty demonstrated that he didn't just belong to the PCB but was one of the fiercest advocates of communist ideals as well. In the 1940s and 1950s, Aristides represented the party at the youth congress in Budapest, defended Luís Carlos Prestes (a communist leader) in court, and denounced the Korean War and 'Yankee aggression'. In the federal chamber of deputies, he opposed the privatisation of Brazilian oil. When he stood for re-election in 1954, *Voz Operaria*, a communist newspaper, wrote: '*Os favelados* (slum dwellers) of the Federal District have a distinguished spokesman in him for their aspirations for a less miserable life.'

His brother João was a Marxist-Leninist who subscribed to the ideology's basic tenet: the proletariat needed to overthrow capitalist society. He believed that education and healthcare should be free for all. 'Like every left-wing militant, João Saldanha believed that you need to do the groundwork,' commented Raul Milliet, Saldanha's nephew.

In the mid-1940s, the party had sent Saldanha to Porecatu in the state of Paraná to support peasants in a land dispute with local politicians and the *jaguncos* – well-armed, lawless henchmen of the big landowners. Saldanha settled in nearby Londrina as a reporter for *Hoje*, a left-leaning newspaper, but in reality he taught the peasants about political organisation, communism and their civil rights.

State governor Moyses Lupion rolled back his predecessor's act granting landless peasants swaths of forested areas in return for a temporary share in the gains. Lupion sold the land to big landowners at knockdown prices, with no compensation for the peasants. With the state and landowners on one side and the peasants and the poor on the other, the conflict was a corollary of Brazilian society. It revealed the deep social divide in Brazil's semi-feudal system.

Violence escalated and the peasants voted to kill José Ferreira de Souza Celestino, a notorious *jagunco*. Saldanha wasn't in favour but accepted the democratic decision. Saldanha relayed to party headquarters that Celestino was killed and tied to a cross with the message: 'Death to henchmen.' Ultimately, new governor Bento Munhoz da Rocha understood the need for a long-term solution to curb the back-and-forth violence. He granted the peasants land compensation but, in reality, the majority of farmers were left empty-handed. Saldanha and the PCB had achieved a Pyrrhic victory.

In 1953 he helped organise the 'Strike of 300,000' in São Paulo. The city was booming, with industrialisation across the metropolitan area spurring modernisation. Getúlio Vargas had returned. Once a dictator, he was repositioning himself as a populist democrat, looking for the support of the working class. São Paulo's industrial workers, however, were sceptical of any politician's promises after the brutal repression of the Estado Novo and president Eurico Dutra's reneging on guarantees of labour support. Inflation was corroding their purchasing power. Across the city, the rank and file began to mobilise: metalworkers and textile workers were demanding higher wages.

The extent of the PCB's role in the grassroots mobilisation remains disputed but Saldanha was a prominent agitator. Saldanha, nom de guerre '*O Souza*', was the liaison between party headquarters and PCB union leaders.

Gradually, the party shifted away from guerrilla warfare. In the 1960s the PCB abandoned the armed struggle for a liberal-democratic revolution, supporting a national front to oppose the military dictatorship. The Saldanha brothers shared this view, which led to a break-up with their close friend Carlos Marighella, who still advocated for armed struggle. In 1969 Marighella was tortured and murdered by the regime. 'Saldanha saw that a recourse [to guns] was only going to feed the forces of the extreme right,' explained Frati. 'The option – the only option that existed was a joining of forces, of the people. It was the struggle of unions. He didn't believe in the armed struggle because he always thought that it was a delusion, a struggle that would go nowhere.'

Elected to the PCB's Central Committee, along with Saldanha, in 1982, Carlos Azevedo explained why Saldanha and the party never again considered taking up arms: 'In Brazil, it had no chance of succeeding because of the army's characteristics. Throughout history, the army defended the country's territorial integrity against domestic, separatist movements. Nor would the people accept a guerrilla movement.'

Saldanha's pacifist stand reinforced his idealistic views. His socialism was both dogmatic and idealistic. Frati said, 'João, like me, during a great phase of his life, believed that socialism would provide a better world for humanity than capitalism.'

Saldanha's transition to football journalism in the late 1950s was another expression of his Marxist ideas. 'Saldanha's choice for football was his choice for the people,' said Frati.

Milliet explained: 'As a journalist, Saldanha used popular language and said that football is not the opium of the people, but instead that it's about the reinforcement of the self-esteem of the Brazilian working class.'

Saldanha, however, was never a journalist in the strict sense of the word. He neither undertook shoe-leather reporting nor chased stories, even if he'd flirted with the profession when he wrote stories for Italian journalist Aldo Saverio's news agency in the 1940s. He covered the revolutions in Czechoslovakia and China, sidling up to Mao Zedong. At least that's what Saldanha claimed, but those assertions remain disputed. There's neither a record of his reports nor of his encounter with Mao.

Clodoaldo said, 'João was like that. He had his stories to tell and he insisted on telling them, always leaving his audience with some doubt as to whether they were true or not. He himself said, "I tell, I tell things."'

His son debunked Saldanha's reputation as a fabulist. 'One day in 1969 my father called me at home and said, "Take all those pictures in that box and burn them,"' remembered João Vitto Saldanha. 'My sister and I burned several compromising photos of him with Prestes, Mao Zedong and Fidel. Mao wasn't an invention.'

Reporting wasn't Saldanha's calling. Instead he became a columnist and colour commentator on the radio. With his knowledge of the game, Saldanha, always tongue in cheek, simplified football for his audience. Through his microphone in the press box of the Maracanã he construed the game in a language that opened up a whole new world to his listeners and introduced new audiences to the game. He was a master in colloquialism. In the 1960s, no radio analyst emulated the size of Saldanha's loyal audience or matched his populist style. His half-time analysis dominated the Maracanã's stands, where fans listened to their transistor radios. 'He was the media Pope!' recalled Gérson.

His writing style was no different from his radio commentary: concise and informal. He delivered his observations with a rare clarity of thought and refrained from the highfalutin language read in the columns of Mario Filho, Nelson Rodrigues and his contemporary Armando Nogueira.

Perhaps there was a touch of tabloid journalism to Saldanha's columns. His truth was malleable. Reality ended at his discretion, and facts were often interpreted accordingly. João Maximo, Saldanha's editor at the *Jornal do Brasil*, wrote: 'He permitted himself to invent stories, portray personalities, subvert the truth and revise history with so much zest and competence that no one doubted a comma of his copy.'

Saldanha got away with it. João Vitto Saldanha said that his father's knack for popular language was 'innate', others argue that Saldanha nourished his skill for mass communication on the beach, mingling and playing football alongside the folkloristic figure Nemen Prancha. That's where, in part, he fell in love with football.

* * *

In 1969, Havelange still needed a strongman to resuscitate the Seleção. The previous two years had been wasted, mainly due to a lack of matches and the politics of the Comissão Selecionadora Nacional (COSENA), an unwieldy selection committee staffed by the old guard.

Predictably, the chaos of old returned. In 1968, the Brazilians, without Pelé, reportedly due to a dispute between the CBD and Santos, criss-crossed Europe on a 15-day tour to play West Germany, Poland, Czechoslovakia, Yugoslavia and Portugal before travelling on to Peru and Mexico. In Berlin, West Germany defeated Brazil 2-1 but the scoreline was flattering to the visitors. Tostão recalls:

'We didn't get hold of the ball, so it looked as if Germany were professional and we were an amateur team. The Germans ran 1,000 times more than us. It could have been 6-1 or even 7-1, haha! It was a real shock. Brazil played with two in the midfield and four in the attack, with two wingers. There was enormous space in the midfield. The next day we were going to play against Poland. In the hotel, Gérson, Rivellino and I sat down and Gérson, who liked to talk, turned to us and said: "We need a complete change. Let's play with three in the midfield." So Gérson dropped deeper, Rivellino played to his left and I to his right, and three up front. There was more proximity to exchange passes and to mark. I asked: "Are we going to tell coach Moreira?" And Gérson replied: "No, he will be happy!"'

The midfield with three left-footed players was harmonious, recalled Rivellino, pointing to Gérson's vision of the game and great positioning, as well as Tostão dropping back to occupy space. Above all it was a recognition that the 4-2-4 formation was archaic.

Even Moreira admitted that Brazil had a lot of work to do. The European game concept was more advanced. In the end, he hadn't learned all that much.

A misfit, COSENA was dissolved. Havelange then did what remains inconceivable when seen through the lens of history: of all people, he trusted Saldanha to become the new head coach, in February 1969. 'His appointment was about rescuing the self-esteem of Brazilian football,' said Piazza.

Saldanha's first press conference was rich in symbolism: a staunch communist and journalist-turned-coach, who made his name by criticising clubs, the Seleção and the CBD was now representing the establishment in a bid to redeem a national symbol.

'Saldanha should have been the last person to be appointed,' said Tostão. 'The political question was weird. Why was Saldanha part of a backroom staff full of military personnel? A communist coach during a military dictatorship, where did that choice come from? And Saldanha wasn't shy to offer his political opinions.'

Saldanha's appointment was a break away from the chummy circle of elite coaches. He was different and, whatever his politics, big enough to not be overawed by the Seleção's mythology. His aura was indisputable: a leader who transcended the tribalism and cliques of Brazilian football. He was the people's coach.

An astute analyst of the situation, Havelange hadn't hesitated to appoint him, even if it led to an inevitable break-up with Paulo Machado. Havelange's decision was a masterstroke because he also took the sting out of the critical press. Now one of their own was the national team coach. Of course, voices of dissent remained, in particular in São Paulo. 'We lost the Seleção,' wrote *Jornal da Tarde*. In the new backroom staff, captain Claudio Bonetti was the only Paulista. He once claimed that he'd 'send my friends from the *esquadrão* (death squad)' after the press.

'In the Brazilian press, the view prevailed that our football was done – that Brazilian football was totally outdated, that *futebol arte* had ended and that what counted was physical football, fast football,' explained Tostão. 'They wanted a popular figure and he had the sympathy of the people, who liked his style. Saldanha was very firm. The fact that Saldanha was a journalist meant that the press would criticise the Seleção and the CBD less. They thought about this. He was a popular figure, who would create a euphoric atmosphere, who'd contain the press.'

The CBD boss bought wholesale into Saldanha – the brand, the creed and the lifestyle, downplaying the question marks that inevitably came with him: his political loyalty, impetuous character and limited coaching credentials.

Saldanha inherited a squad that was raw and unbalanced, a mixture of the old, the unfulfilled and the promising, with the Cruzeiro nucleus providing stern competition for the players from both Santos and Botafogo. The contours of a good team were shaping up but the squad needed a firm hand. With aplomb, Saldanha delivered clarity. He didn't thunder on about shape, tightness, winning battles and other fanciful ideas that coaches believe a match hinges on. He simply picked his team – Félix; Carlos Alberto, Joel, Djalma Dias, Rildo; Piazza, Gérson; Jairzinho, Pelé, Tostão, Edu.

Saldanha explained, 'Do you want to know what the Brazilian team will be like in my hands? It will be a team of 11 lions! Eleven lions, with a disposition for everything and anything, to win. And we will win, like 11 lions! I want more than lions, I want 11 *feras* (beasts). Real beasts! Let's leave the lions aside, their image after those Walt Disney cartoons became a little distorted anyway. There was even a lion camping it up on the screen.'

'He was crazy, right?' chuckled Gérson. 'He said what he had to say and screw it, right?'

'His approach was liberal – one of conversation, dialogue and freedom,' added Edu.

His speech, in simple language, left little doubt as to what he meant and wanted. Saldanha wasn't here to please the clubs or the CBD. His message was empathic: my '*feras*' will play. 'He said: "These are my 11, these are my starters,"' said Jairzinho. '"And whoever isn't happy can pack his bags and go home."'

Saldanha was very determined and radical. That was his biggest virtue.'

His inventiveness and panache were the perfect antidotes to his predecessor Moreira and his lethargic Brazil. Saldanha was straightforward but often quite paternalistic, typical of coaches in the 1960s: introduce simple tactics, emphasise basic virtues and hand the stars on the pitch the freedom to play.

As Botafogo coach in the late 1950s, Saldanha had ordered the team to leave Garrincha his freedom on the right flank. Botafogo players were not to encroach his space but to link up play with cross-field passes, in particular Didi, and crowd the box when the No. 7 reached the byline. In his view, individual skills superseded any collective system. The strategy was basic but it was enough to win the Rio State Championship in 1957. It was his first year as a coach after a spell as club director.

Yet, Saldanha wasn't alien or averse to tactics. Dori Kruschner heavily influenced his thinking when the Hungarian coach exported the W-M system to Brazil in the 1940s. The balance of the quintessential Herbert Chapman formation struck Saldanha, viewed against the lopsided 2-3-5 system that was still in vogue in Brazil. As early as 1963, Saldanha wrote that 4-2-4 had its weaknesses. He applied the system in August 1969 during the World Cup qualifiers, even if there were shades of a 4-3-3.

Those preliminaries represented a first litmus test for Saldanha: could he steer the Seleção to the World Cup finals in Mexico in a style that befitted the double world champions? Since 1966 Brazil had played 27 internationals, winning 17, losing five and drawing five, all while using 68 different players, according to *Jornal do Brasil*. The Brazilian team embarked on a 20-day altitude camp in Bogotá ahead of their curtain-raiser against Colombia. They were submitted to the Cooper test. Developed by NASA, it was an all-you-can-run 12-minute exercise for astronauts to check aerobic fitness, which Claudio Coutinho from the Brazilian army picked up at a conference. The test was perfect to assess the cardiopulmonary state of players as well as their oxygen intake.

In the Brazilian press, the 'astronaut's test' received a lot of acclaim. Rio's leading sports daily *Jornal dos Sports* led with how Brazil were outsmarting Europe and expanded on the Cooper test's significance: 'After crushing opponents from all over the world with extraordinary talent but falling behind in physical preparation … Brazilian football has finally woken to reality – the truth is that science prevails everywhere in the world and the application, with a certain delay in Brazil, is enough to guarantee our players' physical condition that will allow them to overcome opponents with the same ease as in 1958 to 1962.'

Left-back Everaldo ran 3,400m in 12 minutes; the Cruzeiro trio Piazza (3,200m), Tostão (3,000m) and Dirceu Lopes (3,100m) also surpassed the three-kilometre mark, exceeding expectations. Even so, once in Bogotá, Everaldo reacted to the altitude. Rivellino slept badly. Brito, Scala and Gérson had headaches; Rildo indigestion, and Gérson a cold. Team doctor Lidio Toledo said, 'Everaldo was the best in the endurance test in Brazil. But here, he was the first player to have blood running from his nose during the training last Sunday. Other players are also being observed because they showed tiredness after exercise. Others don't manage to sleep well at night.'

'The aim in high cities like Bogotá is precisely to maintain your form and not to try to improve it,' said Admildo Chirol, and he showed DaCosta's *Planejamento Mexico* to the players.

The doctor was happy enough with those mild, anticipated reactions. In fact, Saldanha and his staff almost pampered the players. In the morning, players were allowed to lie in. Training sessions were reduced to a minimum, with the coach arguing that the team had attained a satisfactory level. The players went on promenades at the local golf club, had regular tea breaks and even smoking pauses. They indulged themselves. A training match with Sante Fe was scrapped as well.

Brazil's base camp, Hotel Commendador, overlooking a residential area of Bogotá, was modest with just a single TV set in the hallway but, even so, there were enough distractions for the Brazilian players to avoid the boredom that FIFA's technical report had warned about after the 1968 Olympic Games. They watched the moon landing, attended a local basketball game and Colombia's most famous toreador Pepe Carceres invited the Seleção to his farm for a demonstration. Edu, Rivellino and Djalma Dias were among those who were tempted to try, with a bull of course. Brazil were ready to tame any opponent.

* * *

Saldanha's no-nonsense attitude and team selection were successful. Brazil's World Cup qualifying campaign in August 1969 was impeccable, ensuring their spot among the 16 finalists in Mexico. However, the level of the opposition wasn't very demanding. In a four-week whirlwind of home-and-away ties, they breezed past Venezuela, Colombia and Paraguay, winning six matches out of six, scoring 23 goals and conceding just two.

Tostão recalled:

'Saldanha wasn't a strategist, not at all. He coached in the style of the times – a coach of advice, of personal and technical guidance. He had qualities and he was very worried about personal details. Why are you not doing this or that? Saldanha fielded a team of the 1950s, with two midfielders and four attackers – Pelé and I and two wingers, who didn't track back to mark. Two in the midfield, [that was] typical for football of the past. [There was] a lot of space between the defence, the midfield and the attack.'

Brazil's 4-2-4 simply overwhelmed their modest opponents. In midfield, captain Piazza provided cover for Gérson. On the wings, Edu and Jairzinho enjoyed all the freedom they could possibly imagine. Pelé and Tostão pivoted up front, dropping off in turns. The team's attack was very fluid. Tostão, in particular, thrived, becoming the top scorer of the qualifiers with ten goals, including hat-tricks home and away against Venezuela. He and Pelé notched up 16 goals together.

'Tostão was a "false centre-forward",' explained Edu. 'Pelé dropped off and he would move up. That confused the opponents a lot.'

'He facilitated his own role and the work of others, irrespective of the formation,' said Gérson. 'That was his genius. His intelligence far exceeded that of a normal player. He'd adapt in minutes to a role, with this or the next coach, with this marker or the next one, with the movement of Pelé or someone else.'

Tostão said:

'Saldanha arrived and before he spoke to the press he asked me: "What's the difficulty you face in the Seleção?" I won't forget this. I said to him that everyone insisted I was Pelé's reserve. I thought I could play with Pelé, even if I have to change my playing style a little bit. That discussion of being Pelé's reserve had begun in 1966. He said: "From now on, you are the first name on the starting list. You don't leave the team." That gave me great confidence. It was a reason that I grew a lot. In his first contact with the press, the first thing he said was: "Tostão is a starter." Haha! He had his ways.'

The Brazilians were under the obligation to win by mammoth scores – their prestige and fans demanded it. Some fixtures were complete mismatches, in particular Brazil vs Colombia, 6-2, and Brazil vs Venezuela, 6-0. The memories of some players paint the campaign indeed as colourful and not overly serious.

In Caracas for Brazil's second qualifier, Saldanha refused to allow the players to return to the dressing room after a disappointing, goalless first half. Gérson recalled: 'He threw the key away and said: "What do you want? A fresh shirt and drinking water? For the crap that you played?" He spoke the unvarnished truth.' Saldanha's gimmick worked and Brazil went on to run out 5-0 winners. Away in Asunción, where Brazil defeated Paraguay 3-0, Gérson and Saldanha chased the home supporters. 'At dawn, the fans were messing around, screaming, [letting off] fireworks, waking everyone up,' explained Gérson. 'Before the police arrived, Saldanha said: "Let's end this riot and face them." With him up front, we went to the street and kicked them out.'

The return match against the stubborn Paraguayans at the Maracanã was the decider – whoever won would qualify for Mexico. For almost 70 minutes, Paraguay resisted with some discipline and dogged defending before Pelé got the winner.

It was an electrifying end to an electrifying, perfect four weeks for Brazil and Saldanha. Not everyone was convinced though. A sceptic, Eric Batty wrote in *World Soccer*: 'I cannot help feeling that a team drawn from the Cumberland town my family comes from would give Venezuela a good run.' Batty missed the point. With the team rejuvenated, Saldanha had silenced the Seleção's critics. With the World Cup on the horizon, things were going well for Brazil, almost too well.

No. 6 – Marco Antônio

'That's your third good question,' chuckles left-back and Fluminense legend Marco Antônio, dazzling in his smart white shirt. '[Why did Didi never become the coach of Brazil?] is an excellent question because in Brazil there are no black coaches. I answered you! I answered you! Where are the black coaches? That's even more true for the national team.'

Enjoying pasta with shrimps and a glass of red wine at Degrau, a classic restaurant in Rio's south zone, once frequented by local bohemians, Marco Antônio is reminiscing about his often glorious but sometimes deeply disappointing heyday. João Saldanha was also a regular at Degrau, and patrons, legend has it, would salute him when he entered. In many ways, to pass Degrau's massive wooden entrance doors is to travel back in time.

At the 1970 World Cup, Marco Antônio, 20, featured for 30 minutes against Romania in the group stages and completed a full match only against Didi's Peru in the quarter-final. His luminous, attacking acumen, his greatest asset, had become his undoing; for the balance of the team, Zagallo preferred Everaldo. Marco Antônio was a brilliant player, who could have fostered an elevated understanding with Rivellino on Brazil's left side. Instead, he was reduced to a role coming off the bench.

'On a television show, Zagallo said that I was his first choice,' says an exasperated Marco Antônio. 'So, why didn't I play? Rivellino was the only one to support me. "I want him on my backside so that I can pass him the ball," said Rivellino. I don't want to know if Zagallo is dying. Damn it, why didn't I play?'

It's a question that has consumed those fringe players of the 1970 squad. Edu still scoffs at hearing the name of Zagallo, whereas Paulo Cézar Caju romanticises the entire epoch. Living, all but forgotten, in Batatais, in São Paulo's interior, defender José Baldocchi is grateful and self-effacing. In truth, they're still smarting at their reserve status in the 1970 World Cup. Their names don't roll off the tongues of football's global fanbase, their talents aren't widely associated with Brazil's footballing golden era. In Marco Antônio's words lie irritation, but also genuine vulnerability, genuine hurt.

That pain reveals itself in other ways. During our interview, his family check in on him. Apologetic, Marco Antônio, once a resident of Copacabana, offers a smile and explains: 'Ah, why call me at this time … everyone is worried about me at home, thinking the boy doesn't know the south zone.'

He offers me a smoke, a cheap brand of filter cigarettes. I politely enquire about his life in the impoverished north zone. In 2013, after years of dallying, the Brazilian sports ministry announced a one-off bonus of $47,619 to support, among others, Brazil's veterans from 1958, 1962 and 1970. The CBF covered the veterans' health plans. Reading my mind, Marco Antônio reassures me – he doesn't live in a favela.

Chapter VI

The Salesman

IT'S LUNCH hour and Belo Horizonte, the Mineiro capital, is bustling. Despite the sweltering heat, downtown shoppers and hawkers all seem absorbed by their own interests and pursuits. The haggling is persistent and so is the cacophony of noise.

Shirt drenched in sweat and phone battery low, I feel exhausted. Wilson Piazza handed me the directions to meet my next interviewee, who, when I finally distinguish him, is leaning against a police car, chatting to local officers. 'Dadá Maravilha' produces a generous smile. He's wearing rings on different fingers of each hand, a golden watch on his wrist and a leather pouch.

He seems in high demand, taking selfies and signing autographs for fans and passers-by. Chatty, Dadá enjoys the limelight and engages with all the levity and gaiety of a man at ease with himself. His enthusiasm is infectious, straddling the line between a professional showman and a former football player cementing his local fame. His demeanour is almost ostentatious. 'I invented the nickname Dadá, Dario was not commercial enough,' he says. 'I promoted myself. Nobody did that in football. I coined names for goals and said that I floated in the air and that I would be both top scorer and champion. That was unheard of in Minas Gerais!'

Every minute of every day, Dadá seems to nurture and sell his own legend; conceited but never without some self-deprecation, keenly aware that his celebrity is ephemeral. He shares the fear of many of his teammates: he doesn't want to be forgotten.

Born in 1946 and the son of an illiterate electrician, Dario José dos Santos was a national champion and a world champion who played alongside Pelé, Tostão and Gérson. In 1971 he guided Atlético Mineiro to the domestic crown in the inaugural season of the Brazilian championship. Dadá found the net hundreds of times for Atlético Mineiro, Internacional, Flamengo, Bahia and Paysandu; he claims to have scored 926 goals. The reality, however, is closer to 500.

Yet he's one of the players from the 1970 World Cup squad who never received broader acclaim. In Mexico, he didn't feature a single minute. In fact, he was never even among the substitutes. 'I was a shit *perna de pau* (player),' smiled Dadá, who referred to himself dozens of times as a *perna de pau*. 'Technically,

I was horrible. I didn't know how to pass, dribble or combine. I simply didn't. I will die without knowing how to.'

It begs the question of why a player of limited quality and skill – 'shit' in his own words – was selected to represent Brazil in the 1970 World Cup. His selection became part of Brazilian football's mythology. Dadá, a fringe player, became the focal point of a nationwide political and media storm that would even contribute to a managerial change.

* * *

Dadá has no recollections of his early childhood in Rio de Janeiro's impoverished neighbourhood of Marechal Hermes, except one, a memory that's so brutal and traumatic that he's never processed it. Even as a septuagenarian, it haunts him. The image keeps attacking his present.

His mother, Dona Metropolitana Barros, a housewife, was preparing lunch when she poured kerosene over her entire body and set herself on fire. A human torch, she ran outside. Dadá, five, sprinted after his mother to help and embrace her but, in one last act of lucidity, his mother disengaged. He fell backwards into a trench and from the gutter he watched his mother die. He was crying, his chest heaving, his knees throbbing, his heart aching like never before. 'She had a mental illness, hallucinations,' recalled Dadá.

He spent a childhood in solitude and silence – estranged from his father, separated from his two brothers and interned at various youth institutions for abandoned kids. 'It was everyone for themselves because the older kids wanted to abuse the minors,' said Dadá. 'I had a slingshot and stones. At night, I stuck a knife in their asses. That's how I gained respect. "There he comes, the crazy one," they'd say.'

Crime and violence became not only a defence and escape but Dadá's favoured mode of expression. He wasn't simply a street urchin, he was a young delinquent. He didn't have friends but accomplices. Brusque and abusive, he was disconnected and disengaged from the world. He was robbing for fun. 'I was a thief,' said Dadá. 'I assaulted and stole. I always carried a knife or switchblade. The devil was in me. I had seen my mother die, on fire. What does that do to a person's mind, you think?'

His unlawfulness was an escape from the trauma of his mother's suicide. He was revolted by the world around him. Tormented, he wanted others to suffer as well – and when his own torment became too much to bear, he tried to slit his own wrists. Deprived and depressed, Dadá got entangled in profound marginality. With age, his crimes grew in severity.

Having failed apprenticeships in carpentry, mechanics, tailoring and just about everything else, Dadá enrolled in the army at the age of 18. Recruit No.

7728 served in the *companhia de commando regimental* in nearby Deodoro, but the army didn't bring salvation, not even when his captain told him that bandits had to die. Dadá didn't accept any authority. The result? He spent half of his time in a cell and on the verge of expulsion from the army.

He was released from solitary confinement long enough to defend his regiment in the army's football league. A career was born. A prolific striker, he moved on to the team of Campo Grande, a modest club in Rio de Janeiro, where coach Paulo Gradim told him that he had 800 defects and two virtues: great thrust and spectacular velocity. Dadá has echoed Gradim's assessment ever since, using those attributes to his advantage to become a lethal marksman at Atlético Mineiro in Belo Horizonte in the late 1960s.

His new club didn't enjoy the reputation of cross-town rivals Cruzeiro, the dominant force in Mineiro football, who'd famously defeated Santos in 1966. Atlético Mineiro were about grind and sweat, Cruzeiro about elegance and skill. They were so good that Dadá would sneak into the stadium to scout but above all to admire his opponents. 'Cruzeiro was a machine,' said Dadá. 'I wanted to see how their goalkeeper Raul played out from the back, what the holes in their defence were. Piazza was my idol. He had an uncommon notion of positioning. It was like he hypnotised the ball. It was as if he had eight legs – he dispossessed with one and passed with the other, incredible, no? Tostão was the best player I have ever seen. I simply didn't have the courage to say that. The fans would have eaten me alive.'

Dadá, with his gangly appearance, was at first a fringe player at Atlético Mineiro but, with persistence and good fortune, he carved a path into the first team and eventually ended up in the gallery of Mineiro greats. Dadá was a master of grandiloquence and a merchant of goals, scoring 69 of them in that same year, more than all of Cruzeiro's players combined, he claims. Local media and fans fell in love with his one-liners, rife with both humour and hyperbole. He banished clichés. In public, he referred to himself in the third person. He'd say: 'Three big powers exist: God in heaven, the Pope in the Vatican and Dadá in the penalty box.'

His audacious catchphrases quickly became a part of the local lexicon and folklore. They boosted his self-esteem and helped Dadá establish himself in a competitive and deeply critical environment. No stage was too big for him. Indeed, Dadá, little known outside the confines of Mineiro and Brazilian football, has a major claim to fame: he was a part of the squad for the 1970 World Cup. To this day, the motive for his inclusion is contested. Dadá simply pointed to Brazil's president. He said: 'General Médici was my unconditional fan.'

In July 1969 Brazil's head of state attended Atlético Mineiro vs Internacional at the Mineirão. The hosts won 4-1 with three goals from Dadá. Two months later Dadá netted the winning goal for his club against Brazil in a friendly. Saldanha didn't think much of Dadá and the striker didn't feature at all in the coach's World Cup plans. 'Médici was mad after me when I scored three goals against Inter,' recounted Dadá. 'He was a *Colorado*. He had come to see Inter but ended up seeing Dadá. Médici said: "Dadá has to be called up. He is a machine. You can only mark Dadá with a revolver. You have to shoot him. There is no other way."'

Dadá's version of events doesn't quite correspond with the truth. In his column in *Jornal do Brasil* in 1970, Nogueira revealed how Médici nurtured an admiration for the Mineiro marksman, but there's no quote on record from the general professing his preference for Dadá in the squad. But even if Nogueira touched upon a grain of the truth, his revelation took on a life of its own. Suddenly, both the media and fans were shouting that the president wanted to see Tostão – struggling with injury – or any other striker for that matter replaced with Dadá.

A snippet of information reframed the entire selection debate. Admittedly Médici was a football fan but, in a time when few matches from Minas Gerais were broadcast, it's questionable how well informed the dictator was about Dadá, goalscoring stats aside. After all, his regime had other matters to attend to.

On the eve of a double header against Argentina in March 1970, Saldanha was asked his opinion about Médici's suggestion. He said, 'Brazil has 80 or 90 million fans, who like football. It's everyone's right. Moreover, the president and I have a lot of things in common. We are *Gauchos*, we are *Gremistas*, we like football ... I don't pick the ministry and the president doesn't pick the team. You can see that we get along well.'

That 40-second exchange summed up the psychodrama that was – almost inevitably – going to play out between a right-wing dictator and a communist coach. Saldanha's quote, when read aloud, is quite subversive, and yet on video footage Brazil's coach is seen to be relaxed and smiling as he contemplates his words. His comment, hardly a masterpiece of derision, delivered a singular and decisive message: 'It's my team!'

That attitude and those words, reverberating across Brazil, have often been bookmarked as the beginning of the end for Saldanha; it was, after all, a cardinal sin to defy the regime. But Saldanha's downfall can't be attributed to a single, isolated incident. He was a person overflowing with character and soul. 'He simply said what he wanted, irrespective of where he was and to whom he was talking,' said Gérson. 'That hurt him a lot. That was him, he could not have been different. He said all of this, whether it was going to vex the military dictatorship or not, he looked you in the eye.

You couldn't help but admire him. He had a courage that very few possessed.'

In those turbulent days of media censorship and cultural and political repression, Saldanha was always going to struggle to navigate a vortex of antagonistic forces. Besides, the CBD and the military had always been chummy. Since the 1950s at least, generals, colonels and other officers of rank had meddled in the running of the sports body.

Saldanha was, of course, in part culpable as well. Both his outspokenness and penchant for melodrama crescendoed after the World Cup qualifiers. In interviews with the European press, he crucified the military regime. He agitated against team doctor Lidio Toledo, who'd axed both Toninho and Scala from the squad on medical grounds. Saldanha returned to column writing as well, becoming his own best source and hence inviting jealousy and spite from many of his former colleagues. Much of the Rio press turned against him. A 2-0 friendly defeat against Argentina didn't help either. Everyone was attacking Saldanha: club directors because they had no say over the call-ups; the CBD directors because they no longer were all-powerful; the media because Saldanha was a competitor; and even some coaches because, in their view, Saldanha ridiculed their profession.

On top of everything, Saldanha questioned Pelé's fitness and tenacity. He wasn't the only one. Former

Brazil coach Aymoré Moreira said, 'The problem at times with a spectacular player is that he deceives everyone. His goals have made everyone forget his previous mistakes.'

Even so, a firestorm was brewing. Flamengo coach Dorival Knippel, nicknamed Yustrich, a provocateur, dipped into the moment. At every opportunity he attacked, provoked and goaded Saldanha. A philistine, he argued that Saldanha was downright unqualified for the role of Brazil coach. It was an old argument, often echoed by Zezé Moreira, who called Saldanha an intruder. Referring to Moreira's far-right sympathies, Saldanha replied in kind: 'He is a Nazi and I am a democrat.'

The tawdry altercation between Saldanha and Yustrich escalated and almost predictably culminated in violence, a showdown that was funny, thrilling and foolish at the same time. Brazil's head coach invaded Flamengo's training ground with a revolver but Yustrich was nowhere to be found. The next day, Saldanha, no stranger to wielding his gun in a fit, downplayed his attack as 'a social call that was misunderstood'.

Yustrich reacted: 'We are not in the Wild West and everyone has the right to criticise. Saldanha doesn't have the basics to talk about tactics. He has never kicked a ball in his life.'

Dadá, who trained under Yustrich at Atlético Mineiro, recalled the brawl: 'The whole thing was cheap! They hated each other. Saldanha wanted to stick it to Yustrich and vice versa.'

In public, the CBD was still backing Saldanha, but that didn't matter anymore. A trigger-happy coach was no fit for the national team. How would his team deal with the emotions of a World Cup or respond to falling behind in the tournament? Brazilians weren't interested in the wars, egos and macho behaviour of either Saldanha or Yustrich. They wanted a national team coach with a sound state of mind.

Steadily, support for Saldanha was crumbling. In the middle of March 1970 Saldanha did the unthinkable – he attacked Pelé again, this time claiming that the superstar was myopic, prompting another war of words. Was Saldanha's assertiveness a ploy to cover his insecurity? At least he revealed a gift for aggravating an already delicate situation.

Of course, Pelé's shortsightedness was nothing new, it was an open secret. At the 1958 World Cup in Sweden he'd been diagnosed with myopia of 2.2 degrees in his right eye, but the divergence didn't affect his game. To illustrate the point, *Jornal da Tarde* published a photo of Pelé wearing specs, acting in a soap opera. Alienated, Saldanha was prepared to omit the talisman from the starting XI. Pelé, however, was untouchable. In the CBD's corridors of power, frustration was growing.

In a warm-up match against Bangu, Pelé did feature. Today, Bangu is a derelict club. Their Moça

Bonita ground is one of the landmarks of Rio de Janeiro's football scene, but Bangu's claim to global success, based on having won the 1960 International Soccer League, is trumped-up. Nonetheless, in those days, Bangu were a potent force. With CBD supremo João Havelange in the stands, they held Brazil to a 1-1 draw. In reality, as Jairzinho explained, the match and result had no significance. 'What good was a friendly with Bangu?' asked Jairzinho. 'We were about to depart for Mexico! There was nothing to gain for us. They played like it was the World Cup Final.'

'It was a gift to the Banguenses, like Saldanha said,' added Gérson.

The result was indeed trivial, if not irrelevant, but yet another incident in a long succession of episodes that handed the CBD the perfect excuse to isolate and then remove Saldanha. His outrageous behaviour and inflammatory rhetoric had led to exhaustion. Above all, results were flagging. Brazil no longer carried the momentum of the World Cup qualifiers. CBD director of football Antonio de Passo, Havelange's right-hand man, said, 'The Seleção needs to shorten its itinerary and travel to Mexico as soon as possible. Every day here is another day in hell.'

The Brazilian team was subject to endless uproar, so the military dictatorship decided – irrespective of the result in Mexico – that, after the World Cup, it would intervene in the national game. Such was the official position, but did Médici and his government intervene even before the global finals? It's a matter that until today remains shrouded in mystery.

The feud between Saldanha and all his detractors was always going to end one way. Gérson recalled the last training session under Saldanha: 'He was all smart and roguish and must have already felt something. He was a beast, right? So he gathered all the people in the middle of the field and said, "Oh, they called me to a meeting at CBD. Good luck to you, I'm here for anything, okay? Anything you need. Thank you so much for your time." And he left. He already knew, right?'

On 17 March 1970 João Saldanha stormed out of the CBD headquarters. Havelange had fired him in less than 15 minutes. 'Coward,' cried Saldanha. In the days that followed, Saldanha countered his dismissal with a sharp manifesto in football magazine *Placar*. He revisited the most important events of his 407 days at the helm to offer both an insight and defence of his tenure as well as a critique of his antagonists. His tone was stinging and strewn with invective, calling Toledo 'a traitor, scoundrel and liar' and defending his decision to question Pelé's form, whom he deemed the most exploited player in the world. He emphasised that he'd been pressured to select Dadá and addressed Médici directly, offering him an olive branch. However, dwelling on the reasons for his dismissal, Saldanha wrote: 'I don't know.'

No one seems to. 'He wasn't fired because of the incident of not selecting Dario – no, I don't think so,' Carlos Alberto told me. 'The team's results slumped shortly before the 1970 World Cup. Saldanha had problems with Pelé but it was a talking point in Brazil. Saldanha had gone to the press, saying that Pelé was unfit and that his eyesight was problematic. It was a last-ditch manoeuvre from Saldanha because he knew that the CBD wanted to fire him. He was making a fuss before his inevitable departure.'

Tostão agreed with this explanation: 'So, it was a way for him to stoke confusion. It was never confirmed, but there were rumours in the Seleção, I noticed this, that the CBD top brass were called to Brasilia for a meeting with the dictator.'

Some players share Tostão's idea that Médici and his government ordered Saldanha's dismissal. 'No doubt because he was a brawler,' quipped Roberto Miranda, while Piazza added, 'The military had a hand in it.' Brito echoed both men: 'It was the politicians who pulled Saldanha.' Edu, as well as Marco Antônio, the youngest squad members in Mexico, agreed. The latter said, 'It was the dictatorship that removed him because of his past. A convicted communist couldn't lead the Seleção. That was their thinking.'

'Who gave the final order, I don't know,' said Tostão, with the benefit of hindsight. 'The moment it didn't go well on the pitch they'd exploit the situation.

There were interests for Saldanha to leave, I have no doubt about that. Saldanha perceived that he was trapped. He couldn't bear being a coach and leading Brazil at the World Cup. The political and emotional exhaustion was inevitable.'

It's easy to see why the military wanted Saldanha sidelined. His very presence was a political statement. Saldanha was never going to kowtow to Médici, and the spectre of a communist winning the World Cup was perhaps too much to tolerate. The hardliners, who'd taken over from the more moderate marshal Castelo Branco, must have considered Saldanha subversive.

And the players? They kept quiet. The dictatorship was at its height and the military were overtly present in the backroom staff. When it mattered most, the players neither protested Saldanha's dismissal nor spoke up against it. Some shied away from fraught political debates; others, a minority, kept their views hidden. The majority didn't grasp the gravity of the moment. Besides, the predicament threw up identity questions. What did it mean to be a member of the Seleção? What did it mean to represent Brazil at the World Cup?

'You didn't talk about the dictatorship,' said Tostão. 'There are those who think there were orders not to do this, but orders weren't even needed!'

'We did not have the consciousness that the nation was living under a military regime, but a player should have that,' reflected Piazza. 'In a way, it helped us focus on football alone in Mexico. The Seleção had military all the way up the hierarchy, but a calm marriage of representing our country existed between the military and the Seleção. Maybe our victories reinforced the system the military had been building for years, but they helped the Seleção more than vice versa.'

'We enjoyed freedom on our mission,' said Rogério Hetmanek, Botafogo's winger who'd become a scout during the World Cup because of injury. 'We didn't feel it, quite to the contrary: we were protected by the military. The logistics from the military were crucial. Maybe without the military presence we wouldn't have been able to spend so much time preparing. The government, I think, invested in us.'

'We were made to feel at home,' said Zé Maria.

For more than 100 days the Seleção lived in a bubble, in the facilities of the army, with supervised routines and detailed itineraries, devised by technocrats, all part of a grand plan to mould a high-performance environment as a step on a pathway to victory in Mexico. It was the longest World Cup preparation ever. They trained and trained, and then trained some more in isolation. In many ways they were privileged but detached members of society. News did filter through but censorship was everywhere. The insular sports press focused on the nitty-gritty of the Seleção's preparation, without questioning any ulterior motives.

'The Seleção was very isolated from the outside world, you know?' explained Tostão. 'People ask or think that there was interference in the Seleção – that there was an army environment. No, that is not true. The environment was one of total immersion in the game's technical side.'

'The team was blocked off,' confirmed Rogério Hetmanek. 'The military didn't let information through. There was no outside information to disturb us. You are isolated, you don't think about it. We weren't influenced by what was happening in Brazil.'

The players didn't think of football as a political force and yet the government was hijacking the game in plain sight. The regime's legitimacy relied on supercharged economic growth and the promise that Brazil was marching towards a grand destiny. Football was the perfect vehicle for nation-building. The construction and proliferation of giant stadiums accelerated across Brazil in the late 1960s and the 1970s. Belo Horizonte's Mineirão, with its vast concrete stands and giant cantilevers, served as a blueprint. Across Brazil, circular concrete bowls sprouted out of the soil to stage bread and circuses.

General Médici's interest in football grew. He attended Flamengo matches at the Maracanã and decorated Pelé, after his 1,000th goal, with the order of national merit. Above all, the military's ambit extended to the Seleção. Several of the team officials and backroom staff had a military background or links to the military, including the supervisor, captain Coutinho.

On 1 May 1970, the day of Brazil's departure for Mexico, the head of the 42-man delegation, Brigadier Major Jerônimo Bastos, wrote to the players with soft, oleaginous and encouraging words, but in a tone that wasn't to be mistaken:

'My dear Wilson Piazza, your participation must be seen as the most honourable mission, representing your country, and it must therefore be worthy of and corresponding to the great confidence given to you by the CBD and your people. It's with this feeling, that this leadership dedicates this message to you, in the certainty that, with your patriotic spirit, you will compete for the good sporting name of Brazil.'

The brigadier's secretary was Major Roberto Camara Ipiranga dos Guaranis. In years to come he'd be linked to torture. It's evident from the makeup of the Brazilian delegation that the government treated the World Cup as a matter of national security. 'I never saw Guaranis close to the players, not even close,' said Tostão. 'He headed the security. The Seleção arrived and wherever we went there was a police escort. He organised everything. He didn't stay in the hotel.'

'We didn't have the understanding about the oppression and the torture,' repeated Piazza. 'We were not political. We had little or no understanding of what was happening. We were never told "you need to do this". We went to win, but what happened with that win was not our problem. We went to war, defending the fatherland, and that was going to be used. We served as soldiers, at the service of the fatherland.'

But the claims of the Mineiro duo can't whitewash the players' quiet acquiescence. Did their silence help legitimise the regime? 'The dictatorship was a tragic page in Brazilian history,' said Tostão. 'All governments – dictatorships, non-dictatorships – use sports. History is full of governments appropriating sports. This was just another one. The Seleção was used, but it wasn't the only one.'

'If I had been in the military, I would have used the Seleção,' added Rogério Hetmanek.

'Oh no, about the regime – the political regime, that didn't affect our group because we were football players, we were there to win the World Cup,' said Carlos Alberto. 'The regime didn't matter.'

The captain's words best reflect the non-political stance and modus vivendi of the players at the time. Gérson said, 'In 1969 and 1970 we were there to play football. We knew all that was happening. We were not pressured. We had nothing to do with all these problems, but we went to play, to fulfil our roles as professionals.'

'At a lunch with Médici and his wife, he asked, "Look, bring the World Cup home for me, I am asking you,"' said Roberto Miranda.

Star man Pelé never critiqued the regime. Football simply prevailed and politics were incidental. Dadá went a step further and claimed the dictatorship was good for Brazil. Again, it's easy to see why. Dadá was a product of his time. Brazil was prospering, with an annual GDP growth of 10.2 per cent between 1967 and 1973. In a rich vein of form, the Atlético Mineiro striker was flourishing. Dadá went from the periphery and margins to the spotlight. In many ways he embodied the 'Brazilian miracle'. Dadá was Brazil.

'The economy was booming,' explained Dadá. 'The military dictatorship didn't inconvenience me. I was a citizen who lived with rights and obligations. I was valued because Médici said that I was the best striker in the world, and in reality I was. The president was revolted by Saldanha and his polemics. The dictator said, "Remove him! Remove him!"'

Dadá admired Saldanha as a journalist but not as a coach. Over the years Saldanha became a hero to some and a villain to others. His departure left a vacuum that extended beyond the game itself but the immediate consequences were, however, even more pressing: with just two months until the World Cup, the Seleção were without a coach. The clock was ticking.

Chapter VII

The Realist

FROM BARRA da Tijuca ('Bar-hah dah tee-Jew-kah'), Christ the Redeemer, Rio de Janeiro's postcard image, can't be seen. Separated from both the city centre and its underbelly by a ridge of mountains and the Tijuca national park, the neighbourhood instead can boast of a 27-metre-high replica of the Statue of Liberty, luxury condominiums, tacky, air-conditioned malls and wide boulevards, all laid out according to Lucio Costa's masterplan.

Some argue that Barra da Tijuca is not Rio de Janeiro. It's brash, flashy and the antithesis of a city that recalls the old-world grandeur of Lisbon and other great capitals of Europe. Barra, where bad taste goes unchecked, is a crass imitation of American Sun Belt cities. It's Miami below the equator – Americanised and alien.

It's also a symbol of class division in Rio – the old elite regards Barra with snooty contempt, and the rest can't afford it. But you'll not hear the celebrities and arrivistes in Barra complain.

It's also the place where you find Brazil's well-off footballers and coaches. On a winter morning in 2013, I jumped out of a cab to meet my interviewee in a seaside condominium on the Avenida Lucio Costa. At 82, Mário Jorge Lobo Zagallo, who was waiting in the lobby, remained football royalty. For decades, Zagallo and Brazilian football fed off each other in a wonderful, symbiotic relationship and achieved victory after victory.

Zagallo ignored my first question, but instead expanded on and dissected his achievements and conquests. He was full-on vain. Here was a man who'd spent a lifetime cultivating his own place in history, a man who would tell you of his glories, and would never pass on a chance to be thanked for his own largesse. He reminded me of Dadá's words: 'Zagallo never tired of telling us, "Guys, I want to be part of history!"'

Perhaps he had every reason to be so self-indulgent. Much of his career was a victory parade but, above all, he was the pioneer and the architect of the Seleção's golden epoch. As a player he provided balance, shuttling up and down on the left flank. In simple terms, Zagallo explained that the 'number 10 was a symbol, it was a very difficult position to attain and so I switched to the number 11, where I created the modern left-winger. That was my thinking.'

He accepted his limitations. It was his intelligent introspection that allowed Zagallo to reinvent himself and ultimately shape Brazil's fortunes on the global stage. Unfortunately, Brazil ignored Zagallo's importance far too long.

* * *

It was March 1970 and Mário Zagallo was nervous. A routine day of coaching at Botafogo behind him, he was shuffling around his apartment in Tijuca. His trophies and medals served as a constant reminder of his triumphs, and yet, when Washington Rodrigues, a friendly reporter and visitor, told him the news, he couldn't believe it. He was top of the CBD's shortlist to succeed João Saldanha.

He'd heard the names of the other contenders on the radio: Corinthians coach Dino Sani, his former national team colleague, and Benfica coach Otto Glória. Sani was a novice, but Glória, hailing from a Tijuca family with Portuguese ancestry, had first-class credentials. He was one of the first Brazilians to lead a Portuguese club, architect of the Benfica dynasty and the brain behind Portugal's run to the semi-finals in the 1966 World Cup. Glória had a sharp mind, gleaning ideas from both Flávio Costa, Brazil's coach at the 1950 World Cup, and Gentil Cardosó, Garrincha's first coach at Botafogo.

Not that Brazil per se needed Glória and his Portuguese victories. In many ways, the country had been the epicentre of the game for the past decade and Zagallo, weighing his own achievements, knew that he'd been a chief engineer of that success.

He was among a few professional players from the middle class, like Evaristo de Macedo, who excelled in a sport that didn't befit their social status. Shorn of its early elitist charm, football had a bad reputation. It was the playground of *malandros* (wide boys) and marginals, not of a reputable middle-class boy whose family thrived in the textile industry.

Zagallo had all the characteristics of a great player – perfect mastery of the ball, excellent positioning, a good dribble and a fine pass. But he was intelligent and shrewd enough to understand early on that he was no match for Didi and other midfielders of great virtuosity. As Roberto Miranda put it: 'He was a good player, but he didn't enchant.'

To achieve his ultimate objective of playing for Brazil, he ditched the No. 10 position and picked a role he'd master, reinvent and perfect on the left wing: the deep-lying winger (*ponta recuado).* It was an unheard-of adaptation of the winger position. Chico, Brazil's left-winger at the 1950 World Cup, and other contemporaries simply attacked and limited their endeavours to the opponent's half, but Zagallo dropped back and helped out in midfield. In his interpretation, wingers had the obligation to defend. A noiseless and nerveless operator, he thrived and won the Carioca championship thrice with Flamengo. He understood that Brazilian football was a place where heroes were born. At Botafogo, Zagallo became a part of the club's first star-studded generation that included Manga, Nilton Santos, Didi, Garrincha and Amarildo.

For the national team's left-wing slot, Zagallo overcame competition from Santos's Pepe, with his cannonball, and São Paulo's Canhoteiro. They were more gifted; Zagallo more intelligent. Brazil had pioneered the back four to get extra defensive cover, but playing a system with wingers left the midfielders with acres of space to protect in a 4-2-4 formation. Zagallo's ingenuity to drop back solved this problem. Feola resisted the idea but Zagallo's industry was instrumental to Brazil's maiden World Cup victory in 1958. Four years later, with Pelé injured and left-back Nilton Santos ageing, his contribution was even more vital. Brazil won again and Zagallo's name became a byword for success.

Zagallo always understood how to get things done and achieve, step by step, what he wanted. He led Botafogo's *juvenil* and became head coach in 1967. Along with goalkeeper Manga, he was the link between Botafogo's two golden generations. Gérson succeeded Didi, Jairzinho replaced Garrincha, and Roberto Miranda netted all the goals, in lieu of Amarildo. Zagallo had masterminded this transition and thus cemented his reputation as a promising young coach.

Through his connection with the youth department and the school of local coach Neca in Rio's north zone, Zagallo kept close tabs on any talent coming through the ranks. He delivered a slate of trophies – the Taça Guanabara and Carioca crown in his maiden season and in 1968 Botafogo even won the Taça Brasil. He reinstated Botafogo as Brazil's leading club alongside Pelé's Santos. Zagallo had a Midas touch. He relied on his favoured 4-3-3, still unpopular in the domestic club game, to deliver success. 'He wanted us to play as if he was still playing,' added Roberto Miranda.

Botafogo played with swagger and an impressive frontline. Even so, Zagallo, true to his nature, never relinquished his innate defensive security. Afonsinho said, 'Zagallo was always defensive. In his entire career, two things are constant: the story of the third man in the midfield – the winger who tracked back, that was him, his own personification – and setting up the midfield – the opponent is going to mark Gérson or Didi, that is logic, no? He would pull them back and advance the defensive midfielder a bit. If his defensive midfielder was marked, he'd pull Gérson or Didi a bit back.' The tactic worked. Botafogo were lethal, both in possession and on the counter-attack, when releasing the speed of both Rogério and Jairzinho.

Zagallo loved victory parades and he was formidable at engineering them. And yet, at first, his dazzling CV didn't impress Havelange. After the tempestuous reign of Saldanha, however, the CBD were ready for a more circumspect coach.

* * *

On 18 March 1969, near Praia Vermelha, an intimate and secluded beach at the foot of Sugarloaf Mountain and one of Rio de Janeiro's wonderful getaways, the CBD's Antonio de Passo secretly met with Zagallo. De Passo wasted little time: talks with Dino Sani had broken down; did Zagallo want to become the new head coach? There and then, the Botafogo coach accepted.

As a player, there had never been much stardust around him. He diligently covered ground, selflessly filled space and always served the greater good. But this assignment was the ultimate step up in his short coaching career. Zagallo felt a deep connection with the Seleção. Success with the national team was essential to his self-image.

He was the perfect fit for the CBD. A nationalist, Zagallo belonged to the establishment. In addition, he was calm and reserved; everything Saldanha, the endless raconteur and hot-headed agitator, was not.

Tostão said, 'He was always a very conservative person – in the sense of being closely linked to power, linked to the CBD, the yellow shirt, and Brazil. Extremely vain, but from the technical and tactical point of view he was focused.'

Afonsinho added, 'He never said anything outside of football. He was very reserved.'

'Zagallo was a family person, who measured his words well so as not to offend anyone,' said Rogério Hetmanek. 'He was always sweet and won everyone's friendship, because he had a calm temper and didn't want conflict.'

That evening, Zagallo met the players for the first time and did what he always does in an opening address – review his own career. Then he asked his audience 'to defend and attack in unison', a maxim cultivated by the 1954 World Cup-winning German coach Sepp Herberger. Zagallo said, 'That is modern football, with solidarity, football that is played around the world.'

The Seleção was in turmoil but Zagallo explained where he wanted to take them. He was going to bring deeper thinking to the team. His predecessor, Saldanha, took control, playing 4-2-4, and breezed through the qualifiers against generally weak opponents. The attractive style that pleased the players and restored confidence in the Seleção, however, didn't impress Zagallo. It left the midfield too exposed.

'And with 4-2-4, we had never won anything,' remembered Zagallo. 'We started to win in a 4-3-3 formation, in which I, Zagallo, was chosen to run back and forth. So, when Brazil was in possession, I was the attacking left-winger. When Brazil lost possession, I dropped back and became a midfielder.'

In Zagallo's view, Brazil had been heading in the wrong direction. The team needed quick adjustments for a better balance. And thus, Zagallo did what he'd done at the 1958 World Cup in Sweden, at the 1962 World Cup in Chile, and as a coach of Botafogo: he turned the team into a living iteration of himself.

* * *

A winner, Zagallo debuted with a 5-0 hammering of Chile in March 1970, but it wasn't until the last friendly before departure to Mexico, against Austria on the eve of Labour Day, that his team finally began to take shape. The previous four friendlies had yielded lukewarm performances and even disappointing blank draws against neighbours Paraguay and Bulgaria's U-23 team. Zagallo had his personality and convictions but even he noticed that his team weren't clicking. Out of form and shorn of the disposition to withstand the pressure from fans and media, Paulo Cézar Caju wasn't delivering, and neither Roberto Miranda nor Dadá – classic centre-forwards – were convincing alongside Pelé. Brave and opportunistic marksmen, they lacked finesse.

Zagallo tweaked one position across his defence, midfield and attack against the Europeans. Once the captain and absolute starter, Wilson Piazza dropped from holding midfielder to centre-back, his presence and passing enhancing the quality of the backline and improving the build-up play. He demonstrated an immediate understanding of his role, covering space left by left-back Marco Antônio and complementing Brito at the heart of the defence.

Even so, Piazza felt some frustration in his new role: 'Gosh, I was used to playing in the midfield, to run more, to battle more, to sweat more, so at the end of Cruzeiro matches, my shirt was totally soaked. As a central defender with the Seleção, my radius of action was more limited and grew smaller. After I finished the match, I put my hand on my shirt and thought that I had not played the way I wanted because I didn't sweat as much as I would in the midfield.'

His sacrifice allowed Clodoaldo to slot into the role of defensive midfielder, working tirelessly in the shadow of Gérson. Rivellino replaced the hapless Paulo Cézar Caju as the third man or false left-winger in midfield. The left-footed Rivellino then was playing the Zagallo role, the deep-lying winger fundamental in the coach's 4-3-3. Edu, however, was the ultimate victim. A true winger, he'd thrived during the World Cup qualifiers under Saldanha in a 4-2-4. Rivellino explained:

'That was the game of my life because if I didn't play well, I would not have made the team. I was anxious and nervous – to play in a position I didn't know. I said, "Zagallo, if you want me to play on the left wing I am not going to play. I'm a midfielder, I have always been. What do you want of me?" "No, you will have freedom, but I want you to play with Clodoaldo and Gérson when out of possession." If you analyse it frankly, he put me in a situation I hadn't trained for.'

Rivellino had few of Paulo Cézar Caju's attributes: the speed and the knack to reach the byline. Instead, his tendency to drift inside left the Brazilian line-up asymmetrical. They had little ammunition on the left, with Marco Antônio – and later Everaldo – under orders to restrain their attacking instincts. 'I had an advantage in that sense because Gérson was never a very attacking player, a player of infiltration,' said Rivellino. 'So, there was that space. I occupied the left side of the midfield, always floating. But I'd look at the bench, at Edu and Paulo Cézar and sometimes wonder: what am I doing here?'

Tostão, the final piece in the jigsaw, would sometimes seek to fill in on the left. Under Zagallo, Tostão found himself to be Pelé's reserve again. He wanted his strikers to weigh on defenders, to be a constant presence in the opponent's penalty box, but his preference for a classic No. 9 was still somewhat mystifying.

In the World Cup qualifiers, Tostão had demonstrated his goalscoring prowess with verve. His nous for finishing was no less than that of Dadá or Roberto Miranda, who scored twice against the Chileans before getting sent off in the return match.

Besides, Tostão's sophistication fomented a unique understanding with Pelé. It was for all to see that Tostão was a player *sui generis*, that he could play with Pelé.

Although benched, Tostão wasn't too worried. He realised that Pelé wouldn't click with either Roberto Miranda or Dadá, a conclusion Zagallo belatedly arrived at. Having recovered from an eye injury sustained in the second half of 1969, Tostão was still not entirely match fit, but he demonstrated enough against the Austrians to stake his claim in the team. In and around the box he diligently fulfilled the role of playing without the ball, a sign that Zagallo's team was developing.

Even out of possession, players had a responsibility – to track back and close down the space, to cover and defend. It was a great feat of Zagallo to instil his team with such a sense of duty. After all, Brazil were fielding five players with a claim to the No. 10 shirt: Pelé, Rivellino and Jairzinho, who wore the shirt number at their respective clubs Santos, Corinthians and Botafogo, and Gérson and Tostão. 'At the World Cup, our Seleção must always have eight men behind the ball when the opponent is in possession,' said Zagallo. 'And this is in a normal situation, because when there's a heavy onslaught I want nine or ten men or even the entire team to defend.'

Once Brazil shed the W-M system for the back four in the 1950s, Zagallo's preference for compact football was almost a natural evolution. Increasingly, Brazil had men behind the line of the ball when out of possession. Tostão explained:

'Zagallo had this idea of compact football. When we lost the ball, he wanted us to track back; when we had possession to advance as one. So, it was more or less the model of modern football, with less of today's intensity. Tactically speaking, Brazil was also revolutionary. As a coach and strategist, Zagallo surprised me. The coach of Cruzeiro sat pitchside during the training. He talked to journalists and we did what we wanted. Zagallo held a tactical training every day.'

Carlos Alberto expanded on this:

'Our players were determined to play pure football – when you have the ball, you play and attack with six or seven players; when the opponent has the ball, you have to come back and mark to protect your defence. That is more important than theorising about a 4-2-4 or a 4-3-3. In the qualifiers we played the 4-2-4 formation on paper, but not per se on the field. Out of possession, we simply had to track back. Tostão came back, Gérson defended, and so did Pelé. Everybody had to defend and shore up the midfield, except Jairzinho. He stayed up front and was the point of escape. Zagallo dropped Rivellino into the team, but both systems worked well. It was the same as playing 4-2-4 or 4-3-3 or 4-4-2 for us – when we had the ball, we attacked with six or seven players. The team with possession controls the game.

The opponent simply can't score. That's very important, that you are in charge of the game.'

Ultimately, Rivellino's goal was the difference between Brazil and Austria, but the Brazilians were satisfied with their collective and individual performance, the best to date yet under Zagallo. Both Piazza and Rivellino were happy with their new roles. In attack, Tostão and Pelé, near peak physical fitness, showed glimpses of why they should be the preferred attacking duo in Mexico.

At the full-time whistle, Miguel Gustavo's '*Pra Frente Brasil*' was heard around the Maracanã, a song, propagating the idea of progress and national unity, that the military dictatorship and TV Globo adopted and eventually became the theme of the World Cup. The lyrics claimed that 90 million Brazilians moved all together, yet that harmony didn't exist in the stands. The public's confidence had been undermined by the crisis leading to Saldanha's downfall and the unconvincing results under Zagallo. The World Cup draw hadn't helped matters either. In Group 3, Zagallo's team faced reigning world champions England, 1962 World Cup finalists Czechoslovakia and a formidable Romania. It was the competition's group of death.

'We trained and we had a competent team, but the team left Brazil with our reputation in tatters,' said Rivellino.

'Brazilians just want to win, there is no other result,' explained Edu. 'A draw is not enough. We won at the Maracanã and so things calmed down a bit, but even so, we left for the World Cup discredited by the press and by the Brazilian fans, right? [You thought] wow, are we going to make it?'

Rivellino added, 'No one believed in Brazil.'

No. 2 – Brito

An octogenarian, Brito – full name Hércules Brito Ruas – is no longer the kind of super-powered defender that anchored Brazil's defence during the 1960s and 1970s. He has become frail and almost scrawny, but he still talks astutely and energetically. Sometimes he's softly spoken; more often, though, he's coarse.

It's hard to imagine that here stands a Greek hero in his own right and a star of Brazilian football. Brito was the heir to Brazil's 1958 captain Heraldo Bellini and partner of Wilson Piazza – his 'chefinho' – in 1970. According to a World Health Organization study on the eve of the World Cup, Brito, and not Pelé or Jairzinho, was the fittest player.

On 2 May 1970 Brazil arrived in Guadalajara. Five days later they settled down in Guanajuato, where they stayed until 27 May to adapt to the altitude and maintain their fitness levels. Brito proved to be the athlete par excellence; in February he finished second in the Cooper test behind Dirceu Lopes with 3,140m. His fitness slowly peaked. In April he came first with 3,300m and again in Guanajuato. He was the ultimate exponent of Brazil's demanding preparations.

Perhaps it was Brito's destiny. His father called him Hércules because he 'was born weighing almost ten kilos'. Early on he strove to compensate for his relative lack of technique by working tirelessly on the physical side of his game. After training he'd run the length and breadth of his home, Ilha do Governador.

He devised his own energy drink: a sweet Caracu beer with two eggs, a spoon of honey and a spoon of cinnamon mixed in. 'Damn yummy!' he added.

He cracked up with laughter, enjoying his own jokes. Brito looked much the same as he had in the past years: Brazil shirt, faint eyebrows and a wispy white beard.

His stamina and strength were crucial to Brazil's performance, even if he was never a symbol of stability in the chaos that sometimes rattled the back four. Brito, though, resisted the endless English onslaught in Guadalajara. His aerial game kept England at bay. 'It was the most difficult game of my life, of my professional career,' remembered Brito.

His voice and words revealed his fulfilment in his achievements and victories. His face was mellow with reminiscence, even if some of the finer details of the 1970 World Cup escape his memory. He longed for those days.

He belonged to a generation when footballers were more sportsman and less celebrity. As a defender of the Seleção, he never enjoyed global recognition and renown, but he didn't mind. From Pelé to Félix, the team, in his view, was egalitarian.

Today, Brito is almost forgotten. He hardly ever leaves Ilha do Governador, the gateway to Brazil and home to Rio de Janeiro's international airport. Residents are sandwiched between the stench of the bay, a waft of garbage and waste, and the noise of the aeroplanes. But he cherishes the island where he was born and where he'll die. A descendant of fishermen, Brito always led a simple working-class life, removed from Rio's vortex of insanity.

'Everything on the island is the fruit of fishermen,' said Brito. 'I love fishing. It's mental hygiene. You fight with the fish, it can pull you. One scared me once. When I pulled it out, the fish weighed more than ten kilos, a croaker! There are fish that give you a hell of a headache.'

Chapter VIII

The Real Final

TEN MINUTES in and Jairzinho's acceleration and Pelé's athleticism proved how devastating Brazil could be in a 60-metre move that lasted seven seconds. Two passes and one header. That's all it took. England and Banks, who almost defied the laws of physics, had been warned, and yet for the next 20 minutes little happened. The excruciating heat and the fear of a shattering defeat tormented the teams. Whenever they could, the players walked, the ball at their feet, in defiance of and in subjugation to the circumstances. Off the ball they moved even less.

Brazil probed and poked, but with restraint, proof that Zagallo's team was playing not to lose. Out of possession the Brazilians massed behind the ball, often with seven, eight or even nine outfield players, applying one of Zagallo's key ideas – in the modern game you had to close down space. The shift in strategy left Brazil often trapped in their own half. England's plan was clear: shut down Pelé, keep possession and preserve strength. And, above all, target Félix with high crosses.

Piazza recalled:

'Our concern was height, but at times the danger resided on the ground. Brazilian football was always criticised because it didn't know how to deal with high balls, while European football often employed an aerial game. A cross flew over [Geoff] Hurst and me. I was not going to win the header, so I tried to unsettle him. The ball dropped half a metre behind us. Someone from the midfield or Brito should have been covering, marking [Francis] Lee, who anticipated that cross. But fate was on our side and Félix was very alert not to concede. He saved one on one.'

In the opening minutes the industrious Lee had fouled Everaldo and now he assaulted Félix, with little reason, barging the keeper in his follow-through - a silly and fiddling piece of aggression. Dismayed, the Brazilians plotted swift retaliation.

Rivellino: 'Carlos Alberto said that someone had to hit him, someone had to hit him. He didn't know how to kick someone.'

Carlos Alberto: 'When the game restarted, I asked Pelé to get back at Lee. He knew how to get revenge. Pelé knew how to do it. Piazza didn't.'

Piazza: 'As in life, it is not enough to want to do it, you need to know how to do it. There was mischief in wanting to injure Félix.'

Rivellino: 'Lee deserved it. Carlos Alberto ran in and caught him. He could have injured Lee, but he deserved it because he had cowardly knocked Félix's face. The ball wasn't even in the air, it was in Félix's arms.'

Carlos Alberto: 'Finally, I got back at him, just to show England and him that we were hungry to win.'

His intervention was that of a hatchet man, neither subtle nor elegant, but dirty and base, aggressively body-checking the Manchester City striker. It was the moment when the integrity of a grippingly tight contest was in danger.

Rivellino: 'It was just that one foul from Carlos Alberto. Just to say, "Oi, we are here as well, we are here."'

Piazza: 'He wanted to impose a certain authority.'

Rivellino: 'Carlos Alberto should have been sent off, but the referee didn't do it, because he regretted not having sent off Lee. So he said in his mind, "I should have sent Lee off, but didn't." That was part of the game. It wasn't malicious. The referee didn't make a point with Lee, so he wouldn't here.'

The English were unfazed. The white shirts ran and hustled persistently, covering and checking the runs of Brazilian players, pushing forwards in a 4-4-2, keen on possession, always seeking out the frontmen.

Carlos Alberto: 'From that moment on we were more composed and cooler. The technical level of the game went up.'

Rivellino: 'You had to know how to mark but, in possession, you needed an offensive strategy. The Seleção played with one *volante de marcação* [holding midfielder]. That is how Brazil played, just with one. England had aggressive midfielders and that is why it was a difficult game – and because of the quality.'

England controlled the first half. The Brazilians didn't click, overrun by one of the best teams in the world, or at least one of the best-organised and best-motivated. Those accolades all belonged to the world champions, who at times moved with a kind of regal, easy arrogance – the majestic Bobby Moore anchoring and commanding the defence; Alan Mullery sitting deep; Alan Ball and Bobby Charlton, arguably the greatest player the country ever produced, in more advanced positions; and Martin Peters on the left flank, swarming the midfield.

Rivellino: 'Alan Ball was a very good player, this ginger boy, who was always involved, who carried the ball well, fast. The other midfielder was more fixed. There was a lot of movement and tactical variations. Lee would pop up in the box, a player that was difficult to mark. Really skilled.'

Jairzinho: 'Bobby Charlton! Very intelligent, a lot of wisdom, a lot of vision. A fantastic reading of the game.'

His remaining swept-over hair glistening, Charlton, the oldest member of the party and veteran of the 1966

World Cup, slalomed his way through the Brazilian midfield, letting fly a wildly inaccurate attempt. His sterling industry aside, England's offensive moments were mostly half chances and brief, disconnected flickers.

Both Lee and Hurst drifted in isolation. The whole team seemed arranged in rigid squares, tenacious yet immobile, detached from the final third, tied to Ramsey's system.

Rivellino: 'The two teams were looking to create opportunities and score goals.'

In attack, Brazil, smoother in possession and astute at breaking up compact lines, teased England, showing glimpses of their fantastic talent. Yet, without the injured Gérson, garrulous, combative and so clairvoyant from a deep midfield position, the Brazilians lacked precision and incisiveness.

Gérson: 'I sat on the edge of the pitch because I couldn't sit on the bench, near the dressing rooms, along with the guards. And I was screaming too, right? "Alright! Beat him!" Zagallo told me, "You need to rest against England." I said, "Alright." But it was terrible. Paulo Cézar deputised and Rivellino moved to the middle to take my position.'

Rivellino: 'That is the position that I mastered. I played there my entire life. Even at the World Cup, it was more difficult to play on the left than in the middle ...'

Gérson: 'The team was set up so that it functioned with or without any given player. My injury was not going to affect this. Bon, but what if Pelé was left out? On the bench, we had Dario, an exceptional striker and goalscorer, and Roberto, an exceptional striker and goalscorer. Change was possible. It wasn't about A, B or C or even the collective. My injury wasn't going to defeat the Seleção.'

Paulo Cézar Caju: 'The Seleção's game was collective. It wasn't about individuals.'

Rivellino: '… I adapted and it worked out because Gérson's quality was build-up play, much more so than infiltration.'

Gérson: 'Go, Paulo, get inside the box, those guys are shit! And he'd take the ball into the box! Another thing: the opponent didn't know where he'd go, because he was two-footed.'

Discredited and out of form before the tournament, Paulo Cézar Caju bounced back, and here his speed often alarmed his direct opponent, England full-back Tommy Wright. Tirelessly shuttling up and down, he dropped back to support both Clodoaldo and Rivellino in midfield. By half-time, the match was not yet a classic but gently bubbling, tight and a little tetchy. England's grit and organisation matched the talent and vigilance of the Brazilians.

The South Americans let Ramsey's men wait to return for the second half. During the next 45 minutes, everything seemed to speed up, and the match, injected with more intensity, swung between greater extremes. Within the opening minutes Wright dispossessed the barnstorming Jairzinho, Charlton nutmegged Rivellino and Moore tackled Tostão.

Brazil began releasing players forward. Paulo Cézar Caju's attempt swerved dangerously. However, it was an innocuous sequence of midfield play in the 52nd minute that revealed some of England's greatest flaws. The world champions knocked the ball around, waiting for both Lee and Hurst to move further upfield, thus slowing down their build-up. Reverting to high-ball tactics, the cross from Peters, following a one-two with Cooper, was desperate and predictable. It served no one.

At the other end, Tostão's hurried shot flew wide. Brazil's momentum was building; Pelé darted past four Englishmen before Mullery tidied up. Rivellino released a ferocious shot. It was England's turn to become trapped in their own half.

Tostão: 'It was a difficult and very tactical game for the time, very few chances – Pelé didn't ... a lot of marking. England's marking was perfect ... Bobby Moore, the best defender in the world, was marking me and the dribble – the ball that I played between his legs – had great ramifications, because I dribbled the best defender in the world.'

Roberto Miranda: 'Tostão had a middling game. He wasn't in the game at all. I was shouting on the touchline, "Get off, get off," as I wanted to come on.'

Rivellino: 'The English were hard, more physical. It could be that in Zagallo's mind Roberto would withstand them better and endure. Tostão fluctuated more, he wasn't a bully. He didn't ruffle their feathers. But he was intelligent in his movement.'

Tostão: 'I have no doubt that the substitution encouraged me to play differently.'

Roberto Miranda: 'Zagallo said, "Roberto, do what you always do." I'd take the ball and attack them – on the left, on the right and through the middle. I'd drop back, pick up the ball and run at those tall and slow defenders. I felt that worked.'

Tostão: 'The English knew that I was the support striker of the team. Always moving to and fro, to and fro. I was a reference point, a facilitator for quick passing. So, this also stopped the two central defenders from advancing further upfield. They were trapped by my presence.'

Jairzinho: 'Tostão's view was blocked. So it was an act of extraordinary improvisation from him on the left. He crossed the ball into the box with the right foot, his weaker foot, and the ball arrived at the feet of Pelé, marked by three players.'

Tostão: 'I received the ball and crossed ...'

Jairzinho: '... I shouted, "Give it to me!" Pelé feinted with his first touch as if he was going to finish, to shoot. The three closed him down. He lost the angle and, dropping his shoulder, he rolled the ball to me. He had spotted me a million years ago. It was nothing new for him. Our understanding was so strong. Cooper closes in, I pretend to shoot. He slips, falls, I dribble past him, I come face to face with Banks and slam it right-footed to the left; 1-0 to Brazil! That goal was the goal of the title!'

In those wonderful phases of attacking play, and in a matter of seconds, with little space to manoeuvre, the inexorable force and virtuosity of Brazil's forward line destroyed England. Triggered by his impending substitution, Tostão, the archetypical hero, who always questioned his own powers and merits, improvised, elbowing Ball and nutmegging the greatest defender in the world. Yes, he nutmegged Bobby Moore!

Shackled by Brian Labone, he'd ambled and mooched around for much of the afternoon. Now, suddenly, he weaved, bobbing and dancing past the English, shielding the ball immaculately before pivoting to deliver an instinctive cross to Pelé, revealing his greatest asset, a telepathic understanding with the No. 10.

And then, in the middle of all that glare, of the lights and the noise, Pelé proffered something startlingly inventive, a joyous piece of magic drawing in England's defenders, leaving them slipping around, pirouetting helplessly. His was an improvised dance step.

Roberto Miranda: 'They forgot Jairzinho at the moment that they shouldn't have forgotten him. Jair, so fast, and a dribbler, he opened up the space. It was all about "Pilé, Pilé, Pilé ..." Our attack was devastating.'

Blindsided by the genius of Pelé, the English defence, usually so obstinate and quick-witted, was stretched to the limit. With lethal simplicity, Pelé set up Jairzinho. He didn't have to look. Left foot, right foot, left foot. Brazil's No. 7 was waiting at the end of the move. His finish was perfect, both sweet and devastating. Jairzinho, Pelé and Tostão had engineered a wonder strike, one of the high artifice. Together, they'd painted a masterful tableau.

Jairzinho: 'My goal against England was the symbol of Brazilian footballing quality against the greatness of European football in the form of England. It was a chess game and, in this game of chess, the wisdom and creativity of Brazilian football prevailed over the technical and tactical discipline of the English. Only Brazilian football could and can produce Tostão's improvisation.'

Rivellino: 'That was a moment of magic, something that only geniuses could do. Tostão hadn't been playing well, but his dribble and move silenced the entire stadium.'

Suddenly, with 31 minutes left on the clock, England, neither tormented nor crestfallen, rallied. They accelerated. A sense of urgency buoyed the players and drove England's new attacking intent. All the endeavour, the organisation and the grit they'd shown had been in vain, for England were trailing. This was the truest test of Ramsey's team. Tellingly, the England coach reverted to type, introducing both Colin Bell and Jeff Astle. England, he believed, needed to bombard the Brazilian box even more. At last, Ramsey abandoned excessive caution.

Roberto Miranda: 'They went all out to attack, that was the problem. That's when they became dangerous, after conceding. We dropped off a bit and backed off. We began to play on the counter-attack, via the wings, on the left, on the right. They made things hard.'

Rivellino: 'English football had that vice of high crosses. England substituted. Ramsey put two very tall players up front and there was a cross where ...'

Roberto Miranda: 'Astle was a *grandão* [big guy]. He squandered a great chance at goal.'

Rivellino: 'The ball rebounded off Everaldo, but Astle had been introduced to use his head. He shot wide.'

Piazza: 'That was the biggest goalscoring opportunity for the English in the second half!'

Roberto Miranda: 'From that moment on, England wouldn't win. Our defence steadied, sitting a bit deeper. Do you understand? We were all shouting, but we matched the English – dropping deep, but also transitioning when we moved the ball out of defence.

They were kinda lost! Bobby Charlton was spluttering in midfield.'

In the midst of the mayhem, Roberto Miranda felt a sense of destiny. Brazil dropped off, inviting England on to equalise; those minutes in the aftermath of Jairzinho's goal articulated the details that decide great matches. Amid a Brazilian defence in panic mode, the English had their chance to strike, but they didn't seize the moment.

Inevitably, as the second half progressed, fatigue set in. The Guadalajara sun was unforgiving. Minds drained, legs tired, nerves frayed and, with energy sapped, the teams began to fade.

Rivellino: 'The heat was unbearable.'

Robert Miranda: 'They tired. They were all white, so they went a bit reddish. Bobby Charlton – *toca, toca* [pass, pass]. He pressed us back. But how old was he? So, he tired a little bit. He was also a heavy smoker. He smoked a lot. He was backpedalling.'

Rivellino: 'I didn't drink water, you see. We were very well prepared. I didn't take any water but, my God, the heat was incredible.'

Roberto Miranda: 'Boy, I was in such great form that I didn't feel anything. I didn't even sweat. It was cool. Pass me the ball!'

Piazza: 'The English didn't sweat more than us. No, physically England and Bobby Moore were very good. When you looked at Moore's leg, his musculature, my

God, he was a guy with such huge physical stamina. If he had to play 90 or 120 minutes, it'd be easy.'

Clodoaldo: 'The exhaustion was immense. I was worn out. I lost five kilos in that game.'

Roberto Miranda: 'Lee ran the most. He was the guy! We'd say to each other, close him down, close him down! Brito was covering in behind Everaldo. The *grandão* at the back didn't have the physical condition. A Brazilian player is smaller. Clodoaldo was running a horrible lot. He'd get involved every moment.'

Rivellino: 'Brazil had an advantage – the Seleção was very well prepared. I had never been so fit in my life as I was in Mexico.'

Roberto Miranda: 'I was flying at the World Cup, I was in peak fitness. I ran and ran, and didn't tire!'

Piazza: 'All of this was scientifically planned and executed.'

Rivellino: 'Brazil were always better in the second half. Then, the Seleção had something more to offer.'

Fried and frazzled, England persevered, but without any attempt at carrying possession to more risky, progressive areas in Brazil's half. Their shape didn't shift, their tactical gambit didn't change. They kept lumping the ball towards Félix's box, the chief route to goal in Ramsey's mind. England had no vision. The incessant aerial assault left Brazil in passive control, happy to lurk on the counter. Paulo Cézar Caju tested Banks again with a low attempt, and so did Roberto Miranda.

Roberto Miranda: 'I almost scored. Pelé took a first touch, should have passed and I would have bent a shot in. That's why I cursed him. Damn, the son of a bitch! It was his vanity.'

Rivellino: 'Pelé wanted to win the World Cup more than anybody else. He wanted to show ... a lot of people were saying that he was no longer Pelé. There was criticism at the address of Pelé. He showed a positive, astral energy in preparation, in wanting to win. He was the greatest example I had in my life. "We are going to win, we have to win," he'd say. A double world champion, he was incredible, he was exemplary.'

Roberto Miranda: 'The English pronounced it "Pilé, Pilé, Pilé, Pilé." Were they only going to obsess over the King? "Pilé, Pilé." In the two previous World Cups, yes, alright, but in 1970 he was no longer the guy.'

Pelé, indeed, was no longer the boy wonder who'd stormed to victory and stardom in Sweden and Chile, but a mature genius, more refined and economic, effervescent as ever. He remained the team's lodestar even if he wasn't the formative thinker. His subtle assist proved that the English, whatever they tried, had failed to mark him out of the match. In Mexico he understood the value of self-preservation, the importance of holding back and striking at the right time. Pelé conserved his energy.

Rivellino: 'Pelé was never a stationary player. He always floated around, seeking space. There was the quality [of play] over the ground with Pelé, and Tostão as well. Jairzinho at times would drift inside, Tostão would wander out to the left or he would make central runs.'

In a frantic finale, the world champions were bound up in details of organisation and clung on to their long, high-ball fetish, ignoring the evidence of the past 85 minutes. The Brazilian rearguard defended in a frenzy, near hysteria, stretched thin, paddling their way through until the end.

Rivellino: 'Until the end of the game ... anything could happen.'

Roberto Miranda: 'Towards the end, there was Brazilian *malandragem* (trickery). I'd pick up the ball and take it towards the corner flag where I'd wait for them to foul me. And so I'd say to the ref, "Foul!" That would also hold up play. Haha, and so time ran on. I irritated the English – come over here, come over here! Ramsey shouted, "He is quick, quick! Careful, he is going for goal!" A Brazilian is very *malandro* [tricky], more so than the English. I pushed them – before I'd receive the ball I'd push them. I pushed and would shout at the ref that they were pushing me! I was lying because I had fouled them. It was *malandro*.'

England threw everyone forward. But this meant Brazil had some control. Audaciously, Pelé, less present in the last seconds of the match, chipped a ball towards

Banks's goal and then waved to Abraham Klein, telling the Israeli referee that time was up.

Brito: '[It was] the hardest game of my life, of my career as a professional football player.'

Roberto Miranda: 'We could breathe when the game was over, right? It was agonising, but we stuck it out.'

Piazza: 'The game, when finished, was a weight off your shoulders. You felt light. The winners were always going to prosper.'

The Brazilians were relieved. The 90 minutes had been pockmarked with reminders of their own flaws but they had every reason to be satisfied: the match that mattered most had been won. The momentum was with Brazil and so was the belief that this team was on the way to greatness and perhaps the final on 21 June.

Tostão: 'That victory had a big emotional fallout because I noticed – everyone was talking about it – that those training sessions in the months before the World Cup had formed a spectacular team. Everyone saw that the team was going to be spectacular, it had everything to be spectacular.'

Jairzinho: 'After this game, the written press, radio and TV were saddened: they had already witnessed the final *avant la lettre*.'

Piazza: 'An English player – A, B or C – said goodbye and see you soon! Até breve! They believed there'd be a rematch, a new England–Brazil, another game.'

Rivellino: 'We can win the World Cup, we can become the world champions. That's what I thought.'

Roberto Miranda: 'The onus was on us, you understand? If we beat you, Bobby Charlton and Bobby Moore, we are the world champions.'

Clodoaldo: 'That game really instilled us with the belief that we'd win a third World Cup.'

Gérson: 'Our team was better, it was a team that knew what it wanted. We knew our ability, we knew how the English played. They were a good and a very experienced team, but they would not have won against us.'

Tostão: 'Everyone was playing at their best – Gérson, Pelé, Jairzinho. You could see that the team would flourish. Everyone had that feeling, you know? So when that game ended – England were theoretically the favourites to win the World Cup – the sense in the team was that we had everything to be world champions.'

Chapter IX

A World Cup Classic?

THE 1970 World Cup was the greatest show on earth. Even today the tournament is lauded and romanticised as the end of an era when the game was more innocent. Football passed from sporting lore into pop culture: the Telstar, the cotton shirts, the grainy colour footage, the crackling TV commentary and the matches with a goal average of 2.97 – still a post-war record – all belied that the game was at a crossroads.

Professionalism and commercialisation were looming. The sport was globalising. That was the paradox of the 1966 World Cup: while football in northern Europe was on the ascent on the field, the Old Continent was losing its grip on FIFA. Mexico 1970 was the first World Cup outside of Europe and South America. Sceptics argued that the heat and altitude would dull the senses and thwart a level of play befitting a World Cup. Maybe, initially, they were right. There were stolid matches and stinkers, notably the goalless opener between the hosts and the USSR. In Group 1, the Belgians were lethargic and homesick. In Group 2, Italy navigated past Sweden, Israel and Uruguay in the most economical of ways, with a single goal in their single win.

But their low-scoring group was the exception in a tournament overflowing with goals. In Group 4, Morocco delighted against West Germany, who swept aside Bulgaria 5-2, and the thrilling Peruvians with Teófilo Cubillas in their bright white shirts with a red sash, 3-1. Even Mexico and the USSR ignited with convincing four-goal victories on matchday two, but amid all the high-scoring matches and a timeless all-star cast, including Franz Beckenbauer, Giacinto Facchetti, Gerd Müller, Gigi Riva, Gianni Rivera, Uwe Seeler and Lev Yashin, there was one match and one cast of dramatis personae that stood out, that would define the tournament: the clash in Group 3 between the defending world champions, England, and the winners of 1958 and 1962, Brazil.

In the build-up, the English had fetishised the issue of altitude, like many of the other participants, whose preparations were a mixture of the highly professional and the outright bizarre. Communist apparatchiks ordered Bulgaria to train in the snow-capped mountains south of Sofia. Israel prepared in Ethiopia. Uruguay spent time in both Quito and Bogotá. And so did England. Having attended the 1968 Mexico Olympic

Games, Alf Ramsey was, however, mostly worried about the stifling heat in Guadalajara. Team doctor, Dr Neil Phillips, shared his concern.

The English, if still reluctantly, first travelled with a doctor in 1963, whereas Brazil had already taken an expanded backroom staff, including a physician and a psychiatrist to the 1958 World Cup in Sweden. By the end of the 1960s the English medical team still didn't amount to much. Phillips was a general practitioner, who travelled down from the north to London for England's matches. As a part-time volunteer he took a crash course in altitude, heat, tropical diseases and vaccinations. If the Brazilians had Coutinho and links to NASA, Phillips had Dr Griffith Pugh, the physiologist who scaled Mount Everest with Sir Edmund Hillary! Phillips liaised with academics across England and even with a professor in Addis Ababa. He pondered the use of Streptotriad or Thalazole, two antibiotics, against Mexico's infamous gastroenteritis. He got involved in the development of a sodium tablet and wrote a handbook with relevant medical advice for the players. Phillips's devotion to detail couldn't have been more thorough.

England's preparations also had a commercial aspect. Zeiss offered state-of-the-art sunglasses for the England team, Findus provided frozen food, Malvern bottled water, Gatorade energy drink and Umbro the Airtex shirts. In all, the preparations were second to none. Phillips and England had – unknowingly – been as thorough as the Brazilians.

The Seleção arrived in Mexico City 32 days before their opening match with Czechoslovakia, prompting Zagallo to claim that Brazil was the first team to arrive but would be the last to leave. None of the players suffered 'acclimatisation neurosis'; some merely experienced dryness of the throat and mouth. Roberto Miranda, Jairzinho and others reported, on arrival, a bloody nose and other minor discomforts from the rarefied air. England's training was progressive: from a cricket match to a five-a-side game, from playing high-altitude matches in Colombia and Ecuador to a last-minute, ultra-intense acclimatisation to Guadalajara's heat. 'I was better off in jail,' muttered Moore once, referring to the infamous shoplifting incident in Bogotá.

On 7 June, the day of Brazil vs England, the sun and heat were at their most damaging at 36.6°C. The lunchtime kick-off benefited FIFA's revenue stream from primetime TV broadcasts in Europe but ignored the players' welfare. It could actually be dangerous. A 1953 American army edict forbade new recruits to train in temperatures above 29.4°C. Even so, the English were confident. They smiled upon Brazil's resounding 4-1 victory against Czechoslovakia. The attitude seemed odd, more so because of England's laboured 1-0 win against the brutal Romanians. The Brazilians had been imperious and flamboyant: the *tabelinhas* (one-twos) between Pelé and Tostão, Rivellino's potent left foot, Gérson's cross-field passes and Jairzinho's goalscoring prowess showcased their most devastating football since 1958. Brazil were physically superior in the second half, expressive and fluid. Was it a 4-3-3 formation with variations of 4-2-3-1? Zagallo was happy to call it a 4-5-1.

England had been given fair warning but, arrogantly, Alf Ramsey and his men focused on Brazil's weak defence. Against the Czechoslovakians, Clodoaldo and Brito contrived to allow Petráš's 11th-minute goal. To the English, Brazil's backline was lax and careless. The *Daily Mirror*'s Ken Jones ridiculed Brazil's 'schoolboy marking', but that was to miss the point. Brazil applied zonal marking, whereas England defended with slightly loose man-marking.

'Our method of defending was to position ourselves in zones, cover the space and not carry out man-to-man marking,' said Zagallo. 'If we had gone with high pressure marking then by the second half we would have run out of gas. So we saved our energy and dropped back and then when we won possession, the technical quality of our team stood out.'

The Brazilians exploited England's man-marking, an approach that was simply too exhausting: Tostão moved away from the centre to create space for Pelé and Jairzinho. Tostão and Pelé weren't classic centre-forwards, but they dropped back. From the right wing,

Jairzinho often drifted towards the centre. They drew defenders and midfielders, such as Alan Mullery, into uncomfortable positions. Zagallo demonstrated that he was about more than 4-3-3. He understood the modern game, his team knew how to occupy space, dropping back, which fitted the Mexican conditions that required economic football. Ramsey was no less astute. It was an incredible feat for England to keep possession in the heat against an opponent of such tremendous quality, a testimony to the England coach's tactical sophistication.

More than a simple pragmatist, he borrowed many of his ideas from his days as a progressive right-back in Tottenham's and coach Arthur Rowe's 'push and run' team in the early 1950s. Ramsey wanted his teams to pass the ball. By playing Peters and Ball as 'false Nos 7 and 11' – the Zagallo role – in the 'Wingless Wonders' team, he liberated Bobby Charlton, but four years later, in Mexico, Charlton was past his peak. Even if Peters and Ball played in more narrow positions, massing the midfield and accommodating the marauding runs from the full-backs, England simply lacked flair in the final third, the kind of flair Brazil had in abundance.

At the start of the second half, Brazil pressed forward and Jairzinho's goal was the culmination of loyal interplay and individual talent. They converted their single, major opportunity. The English didn't capitalise on theirs.

Brazil vs England was framed as a game of opposites – the inventors of the game versus its spiritual masters, the defending world champions versus the old champions, Europe versus South America, best defence versus best attack, regimentation versus artistry, enemy number one versus the fan favourites. So many strands were woven into the narrative – but it was always going to be a match of finer details, as exemplified in the opening minutes when the teams sounded each other out. At half-time, the English believed victory was still within their grasp.

When England had to chase the game – and they did so with verve and determination – substitute Astle inexplicably scuffed England's main opportunity. In the 77th minute Alan Ball struck the woodwork. On the bench Zagallo was anxious: this was the ultimate test for his beleaguered and pilloried defence. 'My God, Brito and Piazza, will they hold out?' wondered the Brazil coach. 'And Félix. How will those three hold up? Did the critics get to them? No! The rest of the game proved that we could be champions: a superb attack and a magisterial midfield.'

Astle's imprecision was symbolic of something that's often forgotten because of the mythology of the match, including, and not least, Banks's save and Pelé and Moore swapping shirts after the final whistle. In fact, 'The final that never was …' was a rather ordinary football match. In *Scientific Soccer in the Seventies*, Roger

MacDonald and Eric Batty precisely argue that Brazil vs England 'was a tight defensive match in which neither team was prepared to risk it all, for fear that they lose it all. In the context of the competition, it was a dramatic match, an absorbing match, but in pure football terms it was almost ordinary.'

And in many ways it was – the 90 minutes were riddled with inaccurate passes and sloppy defending from the Brazilians as well as a terrible lack of ideas and tactics from the English, who lumped the ball high and long, hardly the ingredients for a World Cup classic. The fact that both England and Brazil played not to lose didn't help either.

In the end, none of it really mattered: Brazil vs England was a match that defined teams, players and, to an extent, lives. England were on the downslide, on the precipice of decades of mediocrity and self-delusion, ignorant of their reduced global position, whereas Brazil were consolidating their golden age. A third World Cup was within reach.

At Copacabana beach, Jairzinho, until this day, muses about his goal. In his office in Belo Horizonte, Piazza still exults at the thought of having defeated England. Tostão cherishes the match because – for once and for all – it cemented his place among the first XI. Gérson still envies those who played. None of them can forget that victory. All of them will die with it.

Chapter X

Old Demons

THE DODGY pass out of defence, the desperation of the last defender, the slapstick finish from an improbable angle, the bobble of the ball out of the goalkeeper's reach, the slow trickle towards the corner of the net, the keeper who trips over his own feet and almost ends up with the ball in the net.

It was a textbook example of how not to defend. The culprits were Brito, Piazza and goalkeeper Félix, so after 19 minutes in their semi-final against Uruguay on 17 June, Brazil were trailing to a goal from industrious right-winger Luis Cubilla.

Félix later explained that he'd tried to protect his near post, the space Peru had exploited in the quarter-finals. But Brazil's catalogue of sloppy defending included matches stretching back to the first round, so their defence was the object of constant scrutiny and ridicule. The theory was that the Brazilians were always an early goal away from defeat – and elimination.

Cubilla's goal rattled Brazil. Uruguay's central defender Atilio Ancheta claimed the Brazilians went 'white' after conceding. He said: 'He [Félix] just fell down, they were terrified, I could see it in their faces. I think they started to think of 1950.'

* * *

On the morning of 16 July 1950, as Brazil met Uruguay at the Maracanã in the last match of that year's World Cup, Ângelo Mendes de Moraes, mayor of Rio de Janeiro and one of many politicians rubbing shoulders with the team, was bullish. He even declared victory. 'You, players, will be hailed as champions by millions of compatriots in less than a few hours!' said the mayor. 'You, who have no rivals in the entire hemisphere! You, who will overcome any other competitor! You, who I already salute as victors! I fulfilled my promise, building this stadium. Now, do your duty and win the World Cup!'

His hubris reflected the mood across Brazil. With Zizinho, Jair and Ademir in unstoppable form, Brazil defeated Sweden 7-1 and Spain 6-1 in the final four-team group, a bizarre FIFA concoction. Brian Glanville wrote that Brazil exhibited 'the football of the future'. The local media and fans were euphoric. Brazil, they believed, had one hand on the trophy.

Their neighbours hadn't excelled in the competition, even if the Peñarol trio of inside-forward Juan Alberto

Schiaffino, winger Alcides Ghiggia and box-to-box midfielder Obdulio Varela were formidable, if not world-class. To win the trophy, Brazil needed just a point from the match.

Instead, that Sunday afternoon became a Shakespearian tragedy. Brazil could have drawn, might have won, but ended up losing 2-1, to a 79th-minute goal from Ghiggia. In *Barbosa: Um Gol Silencia o Brasil*, Roberto Muylaert reconstructs the strike, dissecting the camera footage. He writes: 'He [Ghiggia] took six steps, in six seconds, not a great deal in world football, but the longest moments of suffering in Brazilian sports history … Uruguay's right-winger ran an incredible 40m without being attacked. Another step and he shot …' and Muylaert draws a comparison with the inevitability of Abraham Zapruder's images of President John Kennedy's assassination in November 1963.

Brazil wept. They'd failed, as a football team, as a nation. Brazil hadn't tasted a defeat of such proportions before. So, scapegoats needed to be found. The culprits Barbosa, Juvenal and Bigode, all black, were blamed for their lack of self-discipline and grit. Goalkeeper Barbosa was the chief culprit. In 1963 he infamously burned the Maracanã's goalposts used in that match at a BBQ at his home to try to erase the match from his memory. The public believed that black people were inferior. 'It was said that Barbosa presented [Uruguay] with the gold,' said Marco Antônio. 'That's why I

Pelé leads the warm-up in a training session in Bolton, England before the 1966 World Cup.

The diagram Lamartine DaCosta presented João Saldanha with before the 1970 World Cup to convince him of the importance of altitude training.

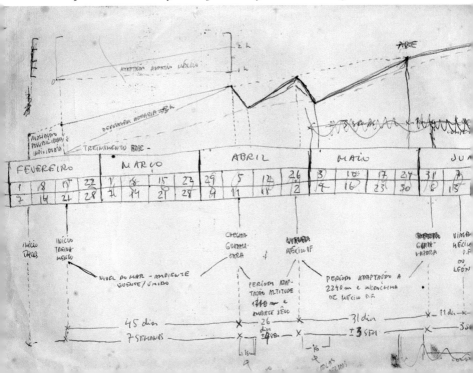

A communist, João Saldanha was Brazil's coach during the World Cup qualifiers in 1969.

From left to right: Carlos Alberto Torres, Pelé, Tostão, Edu, Joel Camargo, Rildo, Jairzinho and Wilson Piazza lining up for their World Cup qualifier against Venezuela at the Maracanã in 1969.

João Saldanha gets awarded the Troféu Estácio de Sá and Tostão the Troféu Golfinho de Ouro in January 1970.

Dadá Maravilha in the Brazil shirt in a training match against a select from the state of Amazonas. He didn't feature a single minute in Mexico.

José Baldocchi and Tostão in training in the months leading up to the 1970 World Cup.

Meu Caro .... Wilson da Silva Piazza ....

Sua participação no IX Campeonato Mundial de Futebol, a realizar-se no México, neste ano de 1970, deve ser a sua suprema aspiração, porque êste é o máximo evento do futebol profissional no mundo

Ela deve ser interpretada como a mais honrosa missão, tal seja a de representar o seu país, devendo, portanto, fazer-se digno dela e corresponder integralmente à alta confiança com que foi distinguido pela sua entidade e pelo seu povo.

Com êste sentimento, é que esta chefia lhe dedica esta mensagem, na certeza de que, com seu espírito patriótico, concorra, de modo efetivo, para o bom nome esportivo do Brasil.

BRIGADEIRO JERONYMO BASTOS
Chefe da Delegação Brasileira de Futebol
ao IX Campeonato Mundial

Rio, 1º - Maio - 1970

MOD. J - 16 - 7/68 - HOT. - 2000

Brigadier Jerônimo Bastos sent the players a nationalistic, oleaginous message on the eve of their departure for Mexico: 'My Dear Wilson da Silva Piazza ...'

Mario Zagallo on the touchline of the Azteca Stadium in 1970. He replaced João Saldanha to lead Brazil at the World Cup.

Brazil goalkeeper Félix makes a mid-air save against England, with Brito looking on.

Rogério Hetmanek's notes on Bulgaria –Peru. He became a team scout following injury.

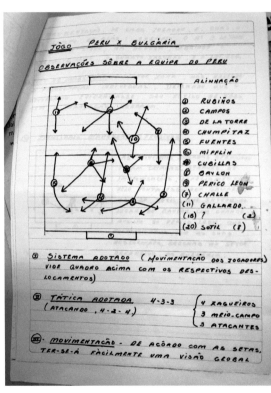

Defender Wilson Piazza despairs as Uruguay take the lead in the semi-final.

Pelé in the greatest goal that never was in the semi-final against Uruguay.

Gerson, number 8, is about to score the second goal in the final against Italy.

Delirium. Jairzinho is carried by fans after Brazil defeat Italy 4-1 in the World Cup Final.

Captain Carlos Alberto Torres lifts the Jules Rimet Trophy. It was Brazil's to keep forever after their third win.

Brazil's President Garrastazu Medici holds the Jules Rimet Trophy whilst standing with the Brazil squad in Brasilia.

Jairzinho, Gerson and Roberto Miranda at the victory parade in Rio de Janeiro.

Pelé weeps after his farewell game for Brazil against Yugoslavia at the Maracana Stadium in Rio de Janeiro, 18 July 1971.

Fashionable. Jairzinho and Paulo Cézar Caju in France in 1974.

tell you that in Brazil goalkeepers of colour are not accepted. Over here, we live with huge hypocrisy!'

Brazil had been the last country in the Western hemisphere to outlaw slavery in 1888, but racism was deeply entrenched and black people were still singled out to explain problems in society. The rise of stars such as Leonidas da Silva and Domingos da Guia in the 1930s lifted black self-esteem, but the Uruguay defeat shattered the idea of a multiracial, confident country. There was no logic to the analysis. After all, Varela, Uruguay's captain, nicknamed *Jefe Negro* (black boss), was a mulatto.

Even in 1970, the spectre of the *Maracanazo* still loomed large. The press recalled the fateful afternoon in great detail. Uruguayan journalists fondly remembered the heroism of their team, while their Brazilian counterparts lamented the defeat but mostly wondered how history might influence the present. 'In the last interviews before the semi-final, it was all about Uruguay and the 1950 World Cup,' said Tostão.

Brazil were trapped. Downplaying the past wasn't an option. Neither was exaggerating it. Zagallo remembered how the match had spooked the nation – he'd been on duty at the stadium as a soldier that day. Fortunately, his players seemed rather unburdened by it all.

'I don't remember the *Maracanazo*,' said Carlos Alberto. 'In 1950 I was about five or six years old. But it was psychological. The media and the fans in front of our hotel began to talk about that game in 1950 – "Oh, take care," they said. "We are afraid.""

'A journalist came up and asked if I feared that the Jalisco would transform into the Maracanã of 1950?' recalled Piazza. 'I was seven in 1950. I lived in the interior in a house without light, energy or electricity. No radio or television. I didn't know what happened in the outside world.'

'Blimey, that [*Maracanazo*] had nothing to do with me!' exclaimed Jairzinho, five in 1950. 'I didn't even know that football existed! It was not a phantasm, because I didn't watch it. You from the press wanted that, you created that. You wanted a phantasm.'

'There was a bit of worry in the team,' admitted Piazza. 'In the view of a good part of the Brazilian press, the game caused a lot of expectation, a lot of pressure. Some journalists were more anxious than us.'

'It's an old rivalry, but we said, "As professionals, this has nothing to do with us,"' said Brito. 'It belonged to a different era. We said: "Let's just see who is best on the field.""

'I don't believe that the emotions of the Brazilians were about revenge, but about satisfaction, joy and, yes, a demonstration that what happened in 1950 was really an anomaly,' said Clodoaldo.

'It was good, because it even motivated us, it gave us a bigger desire to defeat Uruguay,' added Jairzinho.

In Mexico, Uruguay's game plan was preposterous: goals were deemed irrelevant. Preventing the opponent from playing was the number-one priority. The group stage at high altitude in Puebla and Toluca was a procession: a 2-0 win against Israel followed by a goalless draw against Italy in a diabolical anti-spectacle and a 1-0 loss to Sweden. Uruguay had no interest in attacking. They wouldn't have minded for their opponents to grow old before moving up the field.

Their quarter-final win against the USSR was instructive as well. In a 120-minute showcase of conservatism, physicality and willpower they won by the narrowest of margins, courtesy of one of the most disputed goals in the entire tournament: had the ball crossed the byline when Cubilla crossed for Víctor Espárrago's 117th-minute winner? The Soviets were fuming. They felt they'd been cheated.

Zagallo said, 'I never stopped warning my players about the unsporting means they might resort to. We couldn't be spellbound by their tricks and time-wasting. Our players had been immunised against spitting, irritating provocations, improper tricks and vile abuse. They knew what it was like to be fingered from behind in order to get us riled and force us to lose our temper and react and get sent off. It was a World Cup semi-final and that demanded cold blood.'

The Brazilians themselves were far from innocent. They lobbied FIFA hard to shift the semi-final from

Mexico City to Guadalajara and got their way. The last-minute arrangements of an early-morning bus ride, extra flight and hotel without air conditioning left the Uruguayans exhausted by the time they'd settled down in Guadalajara.

During the tournament, Brazil's home was the Jalisco Stadium, where their dazzling football had mesmerised the local fans. The match against Peru was spectacular. Rivellino said, 'Peru asked a lot of Brazil.' It was Brazil's fourth goal in the high-octane quarter-final that illustrated the difference between the two teams. Substitute Hugo Sotil and Teófilo Cubillas were at the heart of Peru's attack, combining to keep Peru in the match at 2-3 against a vastly superior Brazil. As the pair went on the attack again, Pelé tracked back and recovered possession. Rivellino released Jairzinho, who sped away once again and rounded the goalkeeper to ensure Brazil's passage to the last four.

Pelé was incomparable but, dropping back, he illustrated that Brazil's extra man in midfield was crucial in their 4-3-3 formation. Zagallo had moved with the times, Peru's coach Didi hadn't. Bold and intelligent, he copied Brazil's 4-2-4 formation from the Sweden World Cup. From a tactical point of view, Brazil 1970 had outplayed Brazil 1958.

The Brazilians were flying but that momentum dissipated completely when facing a Uruguay that harnessed all their cunning and dark arts to thwart

Brazil, milking the history, the rivalry, the role of victim, the mind games and the pressure. They played with a degree of opportunism that concealed the limitations of their squad. The team didn't have a recognised striker but were soon in the lead. Cubilla's goal cast further doubt over Brazil's backline.

'The Seleção was losing itself a bit in the first half,' said Piazza.

'The good part was that it happened early on,' said Brito. 'Otherwise, we would have been toast.'

Brito and the Brazilian backline didn't cover themselves in glory for much of the tournament. They conceded goals in slow motion, bungling and reinforcing the idea that Brazilians didn't know how to defend. The scenario was nearly always the same: a cluster of Brazilians in and around the box somehow allowing the opponents to wriggle a way through – Clodoaldo and Brito had done so against Czechoslovakia's Petráš; Brito, Piazza and Carlos Alberto against Romania's Florea Dumitrache; and Carlos Alberto and Everaldo against Peru's Alberto Gallardo and Cubillas. Goalkeeper Félix was also complicit, flapping at high crosses or attempts from tight angles. Too often, improbable shots squeezed past him. Félix was no fitting heir to Gilmar. Brazil's defence was wobbly. In some quarters, Félix was considered the tournament's worst goalkeeper. Piazza was a makeshift centre-back and Brito, his partner in crime, was hardly a new Bellini. Full-backs Carlos

Alberto and Everaldo, condemning the talented Marco Antônio to the bench, balanced each other out.

'Did we have our difficulties?' asked Clodoaldo. 'Yes, we did.' But he quickly leaped to his colleagues' defence, not shying away from hyperbole:

'We had some doubts in terms of the goalkeeper, but Félix enjoyed a fantastic championship. When it was needed, he showed why he was the goalkeeper of the Brazilian team. And when he made a mistake, any goalkeeper would have made that mistake, even the best one in the world. Carlos Alberto's defending was the best in the world, there has been nothing like it. On the opposite side, Everaldo was more defensive. He had his limitations, but was efficient. Piazza had a lot of fighting spirit. That was surprising because he didn't have the right stature for it. He had the support of Brito, a fantastic player, both in combat and when covering, and especially in the air. He was our response to the long ball game.'

Félix and his defence had obvious limitations but accusations that Brazil didn't understand how to defend were silly and fitted the stereotype that they were totally committed to attacking. Brazil pioneered the back four and provided the blueprint for the modern-day full-back. They had a superior defensive record to England in World Cup history. In Mexico they played with zonal marking, Zagallo's masterstroke to conserve energy in the heat.

The man-marking Uruguayans raced after their opponents. It was exhausting but, in the first half, it worked. Brazil were paralysed. Uruguay always had a man waiting – to mark, tackle and sniff out any danger. Physical, disciplined and organised, they were doing everything right. It was a textbook display of how the Celeste played – and had been playing for years. They were clear in their strategy and at their best when the call for heroism was most pressing.

Did the Uruguayans crack the code to beat Brazil? Against an everyday team, they might have. In fact, Brazil were enduring their worst 45 minutes of the tournament. Insipid, lethargic and leaden-footed – or 'unrecognisable' as Clodoaldo put it; a result of how Uruguay had set up. Their every move was based on how Brazil played. They marked Gérson out of the game, denied Pelé space and constantly shadowed Jairzinho.

'They could hand it out!' exclaimed Jairzinho. 'They were violent, they caught us constantly. They battered us. Pelé, Tostão and Rivellino got the shit kicked out of them. Some players are evil, like Uruguay's defenders.'

'They tried to provoke Pelé and Jairzinho,' said Piazza. 'Uruguay imposed themselves through their marking, using all their power. They were always a combative side because of the rivalry, as our neighbours. I broke my leg in a friendly against Uruguay. Their players are tougher, more violent, even staunchly so. Their fervour exceeds the limits. Uruguay tried to scare Brazil.'

Pelé, who elbowed Dagoberto Fontes out of revenge, said the Uruguayans played 'as if there was no referee on the field'.

They might have been crabby and cynical but the Uruguayans also wanted the ball, without ever really taking the game to the Brazilians, the way the English had done in the group phase. They controlled the first half, much to the exasperation of Zagallo, who, on the bench, was fretting, almost dumbstruck because of the 'apathy' of his team. Uruguay, in his words, were truly 'like a ghost in a light-blue shirt'.

'Everyone said that "no, we're not thinking about that [1950]", but on the field, it had a big influence, especially in the first half,' said Clodoaldo. Brazil's No. 5 – 'our protector' according to Brito – was enduring a torrid first half, guilty of loose passing and offering little going forward, much in the image of his team. Then, with all but the last attack of a neurotic first half, Clodoaldo and the Brazilians for the first time could see a way through the thicket of light-blue shirts. For the first time the omnipresent Roberto Matosas failed to mop up. Clodoaldo infiltrated, got on the blindside of his marker and wrapped his foot around Tostão's exquisite assist with the same extraordinary precision and subtlety, and equalised.

Clodoaldo's first goal for the Seleção wasn't a coincidence but the consequence of a tactical switch, as Gérson explained:

'On the field, it wasn't going well. I heard [Uruguay's] coach yell to Castillo to stick to me, to not let me go. In truth, we played like shit in the first half. We were standing still and I could hear him yell. I'd run here and there, but he [Castillo] was just glued to me. I was tightly marked. I said, "Clodoaldo, you start doing my part, I'll do yours and he will follow me. I'll drag him here and you won't be marked." We tweaked Zagallo's formation. "Carlinhos, you need to push up." It was all connected. "Tostão, move." He'd take his marker with him and create space to exploit. Zagallo gave us that freedom.'

Brazil were back in the match, although at half-time nothing was settled. It was time for introspection but an incensed and emotional Zagallo – his middle name is Lobo, wolf – simply berated his players. It was the only time during the competition that he lost his cool. He cursed and yelled: 'What's going on? Do you think you're going to lose to that team? The Uruguayans are useless! It's embarrassing seeing you walk off the pitch with your heads bowed. They should be trembling, not you!'

Gérson said, 'Carlos Alberto and Zagallo were mad in the dressing room: "You have to be careful with these guys. They are banking on getting you sent off." All of us wanted to retaliate. Uruguay were beating the hell out of us for the entire game.'

Roberto Miranda downplayed Zagallo's anger though, 'His half-time talk was never really a scolding. Zagallo hardly ever cursed. That wasn't his style. He simply said, "This is not possible." He knew the team he had at his disposal.'

Jairzinho said, 'Zagallo told us to remain calm. We accepted to get kicked by them and they kept going in hard, dishing it out.'

Juan Mujica swept Jairzinho's feet from under him, Luis Ubiña floored Pelé, and Castillo felled Clodoaldo, but in the second half these had become acts of desperation, last flickers of resistance from the Uruguayans, who tired in the heat, even more so due to their extra time against the USSR. Clodoaldo's goal had changed the dynamic. Buttressed by a revitalised midfield, Brazil's attack was a torrent that few teams on the planet could live with. Gérson was finding the space Cortés had previously denied him. Pelé was central to every dangerous attack. Jairzinho was running into promising positions.

The Brazilians reduced Uruguay to the laborious, tedious team they'd been throughout the tournament. A yellow streak, Jairzinho was racing away again. He scored Brazil's second, Rivellino the third following an elegant assist from the clairvoyant Pelé, who played with a fabulous élan. He was in one of his moods.

Arthur Hopcraft and Hugh McIlvanney wrote in *World Cup '70*:

'At the heart of Pelé's game is a joyful pursuit of the impossible. He has dominated the mythology of world football as no man before him ever did, scoring a thousand goals and creating ten thousand moments of exhilarating beauty. He does not hide the insistent desire to score one goal that will stand apart from all the others, a goal that will be impossible until he makes it possible, one that nobody else can emulate: Pelé's goal.'

That Pelé goal eluded him against Uruguay but he produced two unforgettable near-misses, drilling an audacious half-volley at goalkeeper Ladislao Mazurkiewicz and fooling Uruguay's No. 1 with an ingenious dummy. He clutched his face, rueful and in disbelief that he hadn't scored. But the beauty of those moments illustrated how Brazil reshaped the match. The Brazilians were flushed with a kind of affirmation and belief that no matter what Italy would do in the final, it wouldn't be enough.

Chapter XI

The Perfect Win

FOR THE first time, Gérson de Oliveira Nunes runs out of words. Wearing a polo shirt, a golden necklace and some bracelets, he ponders my question: 'Did you control the final against Italy?' His verbosity and authority desert him. Gérson rarely falls silent. A wellspring of energy and opinions, he never stops talking. *Papagaio* (parrot) is his nickname, after all. Sometimes he emphasises his argument by adding *ta certo?* or *pronto* at the end of a sentence – Got it? Done! On Instagram, he even makes his points shouting through a megaphone or, theatrically, by shredding team sheets. *Ta certo?*

In the end, his answer is neither here nor there – a modest 'yes, but no', not taking away the merits of the team, while not downplaying his own role. 'One way or the other, I think yes,' concedes Gérson. 'In the other games, there were also *lancamentos*, defining long passes. I could consider myself the best player in that game, the World Cup Final. I did my bit, in all the games. That's what I had to do. I didn't do anything more or anything less. I was one of the pieces of the puzzle. *Pronto.*'

It's an unassuming view of an afternoon and a sunlit spectacle at the Azteca Stadium that crowned Brazil as the spiritual masters of the game. After all, Brazil and Italy had twice conquered the World Cup and the winner was to take the Jules Rimet Trophy home forever.

The enigmatic brain of the team and Zagallo's lieutenant on the field, Gérson dominated the tournament's showpiece match. With his great technique and intelligence, the No. 8 orchestrated Brazil's play from deep in the midfield. He was a thinker, in the line of Zizinho and Didi, and a supreme tactician. In the whole of Mexico, no one had a more influential left foot.

The Italians also played a part in Gérson's man-of-the-match performance because they made the pitch enormous and failed to mark the midfielder. It was an unforgivable and naive mistake. Had they not analysed the semi-final, where the formidable Uruguayans marked Gérson out of the game? To give Gérson space was to give Brazil the match.

In that sense, his injury against England was perhaps a blessing in disguise for Brazil. The English played high up the pitch, and in tight spaces Gérson's

influence would have been depleted. He dismissed
the accusation that he was too slow to flourish against
the very best, who'd bully him on the ball. 'Don't you
think I freed myself?' asked Gérson. 'Don't you think
that I didn't search for a position to operate in without
too many Italians around? I had to look for a better
position to not be so tightly marked. They didn't see it.
They thought they could play toe to toe with us. That
was excellent for us because we had our plan and our
variations. *Ta certo?*'

His positioning tricked the Italians into believing
there was little need to mark him. How wrong they
were. Gérson was playing a clever waiting game, almost
restrained in the first half, but he saw the opening when
it came. In the 66th minute, Jairzinho was skating
past opponents with ease and elegance, stretching the
Italians thin, as he did the entire afternoon, dragging
Fachetti out of position, even drifting in from the left.
Near the edge of the box, the No. 7 left the ball at the
feet of the patient Gérson, in between Italy's tightly knit
defensive lines. His angled strike and exact placement of
the ball into the bottom corner reflected the perfection
he attained with his left foot. Taking two little taps to
the left, he'd exploited the narrowest of gaps.

'Jairzinho came to the left to drag Fachetti with
him because they man-marked,' recalled Gérson.
'He took the ball on the left and I ran towards him
to distract his marker. Jairzinho ran past me with his

marker and left the ball, taking his marker with him, opening up the space for me. I nudged the ball and noticed the goalkeeper coming out a bit and shot. It was all a moment of instinct, speed, vision.'

It was a goal that befit Gérson. At 29 and balding, he had something stately, his languid movement was magnificent, his stride regal, his competence singular. Knowing the pathway to goal, his brain raced to conjure up a goalscoring matrix, sculpting the perfect arc for his shot. The goal brought recognition for Gérson, the team's midfield metronome. He wasn't the greatest player of all time and yet he was more important to the team than Pelé, who excelled in the final as well. Gérson devoted himself to expanding space.

Carlos Alberto explained:

'Pelé was the best player, but Gérson was the secret to our team playing well. Pelé was great, the best, but at the time, in our team, it was Gérson, and I have always said that. Gérson was the key. Every move started with Gérson. When we gained possession, we passed the ball to Gérson for him to start the attack. He distributed play in a very intelligent manner.'

Tostão confirmed this view:

'On the field, Gérson was the captain. Gérson was a thinker. He was the best midfielder that I have seen because of his intelligence and observation. It was as if he were a coach on the field, as if he were playing from the stands. He guided you a lot. Everyone remembered him as a great passer of the ball. He had such an influence on the collective capacity that he oriented the defenders. He'd say, "*Fulano* (so and so), you will receive the ball there, *Fulano*, come over here." He was a coach. Gérson was, at the time, super-fanatical about all the details of the training and tactics. Gérson was the type who, once training had ended, wanted to discuss it back at the hotel. That kind of guy, haha! Everyone would be tired, but he still wanted to talk. He liked to discuss things.'

'He was the link-up man,' added Jairzinho.

'He wasn't a goalscorer, he was an organiser,' said Tostão. 'A Cruyff type.'

But Gérson's rare goal – his only one in the tournament and Brazil's second in the final – split the afternoon in two. Destinies were diverging: the Brazilians were 24 minutes away from becoming world champions; the Italians were fading, dragging their aching limbs through more gruelling minutes after their epic semi-final win against West Germany. They did have a plan: catenaccio, but they were now nibbling at Gérson's ankles. Before kick-off, coach Ferruccio Valcareggi told his players they had nothing to fear. How wrong he was. Sandro Mazzola recalled Italy's trepidation: during the national anthem, the words wouldn't come out of the players' mouths.

Italy's problems, however, ran much deeper. They were conspicuously naive for a team obsessed with tactical theory and proffered a catalogue of blunders: they man-marked, tasked midfielder Mario Bertini to shadow Pelé and played, again, without their golden boy, Gianni Rivera of AC Milan. The breakdown between Valcareggi and Rivera darkened much of Italy's campaign in Mexico and went right to the heart of Italy's conundrum: how attacking should they play?

In a classic *staffetta* (relay), Italian coaches rotate two brilliant players of similar characteristics instead of playing them together. Rivera was pitted against Mazzola, a lifelong Inter Milan player. Valcareggi decided that the pair couldn't play together because Rivera was too attacking. The Milan player also didn't adapt well to the Mexican conditions. Superb defensively, Mazzola was limited going forward. Often, Italy, like Uruguay, didn't seem to know how to move forward, how to bring the ball up the pitch. Perhaps they didn't want to. Italy's two most advanced players, Gigi Riva and Roberto Boninsegna, hardly moved ahead of the ball.

Valcareggi's choice of Mazzola was a vote of confidence in his team's defensive abilities, in the simplistic belief that Italy could stop the Brazilian forwards. In the 19th minute, Pelé rubbished that theory when he rose with superb athleticism in behind Tarcisio Burgnich to steer a header past goalkeeper Enrico Albertosi to score Brazil's 100th goal in World Cup history; 1-0. Beaten in the air, Burgnich fell at

Pelé's feet. Years later, he'd recall that moment: 'I told myself before the game, he's made of skin and bones just like everyone else – but I was wrong.'

The Brazilians were still mortal, yet keeping possession to exhaust Italy. They pinged the ball left and right, often circulating it in the centre of the pitch, where they enjoyed numerical superiority. To drag the Italians out of position, Rivellino moved infield. The Seleção's restraint held great promise for the second half. Zagallo's plan worked almost to perfection, notwithstanding a quintessential moment of insouciance in the Brazilian defence when a nonchalant, blind back-flick from Clodoaldo allowed Boninsegna to race through and equalise in the 37th minute, with Brito's mistimed challenge taking out Félix in a farcical melee. 'Não, Clôdo. Não, Clôdo,' yelled Brazilian TV commentator Walter Abrahão. Clodoaldo's brain fade was 'madness' according to Zagallo, 'silly' in Brito's view and a mere 'accident' in Jairzinho's opinion.

'Do you remember the goal from Italy well?' asked Jairzinho. 'He didn't lose a single ball later on. The Italian attack didn't do anything anymore. Clodoaldo was so enthusiastic with that back-heel – before he would dribble three Italians! The ball fell between Brito and Boninsegna, who won and scored, but Italy was totally dominated. We totally dominated Italy!'

Strangely, indeed, the equaliser did little to lift Italy's spirits. The Azzurri remained cagey, a reduced version of the team that had showed flashes of attacking genius against both Mexico and West Germany when Valcareggi finally brought on Rivera. But Italy's ploy of getting Mazzola to run himself ragged and then bringing on his replacement was doomed to fail against Brazil.

Tostão said:

'At the end of the first half, the conversation in the dressing room went that the Italians were already tired and that in the second half it would be easier. This was not just because of the game against Germany, because of the type of game. Italy marked individually. Where one player went, the other followed him. And that is very tiring, very exhausting. Nobody can run after a player for two halves. Brazilian players loved to play against teams who man-marked.'

Brito confirmed this, saying:

'Our team was growing stronger and they were fading. Their heads were dropping because they saw it too: "Gee, the guys have been playing at the same pace since the beginning of the game and we can't take it." So that was it. Let's pop them. They weren't going to hold out. And us? The more we played, the more quality we had. Modesty aside, and without wanting to belittle our opponents, we prepared ourselves. We were ready, to run for 90 minutes.'

At the limits of their strength, the second half was a war of attrition for the Italians. They sat back, held their position and let their opponents have the ball. It wasn't the way to combat Brazil. In midfield, Gérson remained free. Brito said, 'They thought he was a slow player and didn't score. So they left him alone, gave him his freedom.'

Gérson and Brazil exploded, playing with a pervasive sense of their own destiny. The No. 8 was the architect of Brazil's third goal, in the 71st minute, capitalising once more on his telepathic understanding with Pelé and Jairzinho. His precise laser-like diagonal pass was the result of years of painstaking training, drilling balls towards athletic hurdles placed in the semi-circle of the penalty box. 'I had to put the ball down there, inside the hurdle,' said Gérson. 'That's not easy! It's only a metre this way, or that way. I had an understanding with Jairzinho. He didn't need to look at me, nor I at him. And, nor did I even need to know what he was going to do.'

Jairzinho would take two steps back to draw his marker with him, the signal for Gérson to launch a diagonal pass. Anticipating the ball, Jairzinho cruised past his opponent to meet it. And he did – because the ball always arrived where it was supposed to. 'Gérson didn't simply launch long passes, but accurate long passes, using all his knowledge, to Pelé and me, two players of a high technical level.'

With a delicate header, Pelé, beating Burgnich again, cushioned Gérson's lofted pass down into the path of Jairzinho, who with a bit of fortune walked the ball into the net for 3-1. Arms aloft, he wheeled away in celebration before sinking to his knees in prayer. With six goals in six matches, he'd become the first player to score in every round of the World Cup, discounting France's Just Fontaine in 1958 and Uruguay's Ghiggia in 1950, who hadn't played in the final. He was 'the happiest man in the world!' yelled the BBC commentator.

The Brazilians were now liberated, a levity filling their souls, a gaiety suffusing their play. At this point, the final's outcome was inevitable. The Italians weren't even downhearted. They benevolently accepted being up against a force they couldn't quite match. A superhuman team indulging in a joyful game – and they were about to display a final, brilliant sparkle of artistry.

Gérson played almost no part in it but Brazil's fourth goal was no less beautiful – for what it meant, for what it symbolised. Carlos Alberto explained how the goal was pre-planned:

'If Jairzinho moved to the other wing, Fachetti was always going to follow him. It happened only once in the entire match, but we took advantage of it. They offered us a boulevard to go forward and score. Pelé was ready to pass the ball. It was at the end of the game and that goal killed any kind of hope that Italy harboured to try and draw. That goal sealed our win. I had been thinking of scoring throughout the entire tournament.

That it happened in the final made me ecstatic. It was a goal destined to stay in football's memory because of the way it was created. We had touched the ball 26 times before I received Pelé's pass. In celebration, we shouted a lot of bad words behind the Italian goal, but that was out of happiness and relief.'

All the swearing was a mix of euphoria, fulfilment and triumph after long months of bottled-up anguish and tension. The electrifying denouement was too much for some. Overwrought by emotion, Tostão and Piazza played the last minutes of the final in tears. 'I played the last moments of the final crying,' said Tostão. 'It was something unforgettable. Spectacular.'

Carlos Alberto's goal came to define Brazilian football. It was Tostão who'd chased the ball all the way back from up front. He recovered possession, before Clodoaldo, with dazzling footwork, dribbled past a Praetorian Guard of Italians, tying Rivera, Angelo Domenghini, Giancarlo De Sisti and Antonio Juliano up in knots. He passed to Rivellino, who found Jairzinho with a delicate pass. Cutting inside from the left, Jairzinho dragged Fachetti out of position. The observant Tostão, taking Italian libero Cera out of the game near the box, was pointing out all that Pelé had to do next. The No. 10 sensed it too. Right foot, left foot, right foot. He needn't look. And even the gods were helpful: the ball sat up for Carlos Alberto to meet Pelé's assist at the perfect moment. It was with thunder that he struck the Telstar. The goal was football ecstasy, the pièce de résistance of a team that transcended the game. This was Brazil's most definite victory.

'That last goal was divine,' mused Rivellino. 'It was something divine to crown our team. We will never see something like it again.'

The strike was the culmination of arguably the finest team move in football history and encompassed, along with Brazil's many other virtues, a sense of innocence. In the context of the match itself, the goal no longer mattered: the Italians were already on their knees. Carlos Alberto's strike was Brazil's 12th second-half goal in Mexico. 'If we had played ten World Cup finals, we would have won nine and drawn one, taking that one to penalties,' said Gérson. 'At that World Cup, no one would have beaten us.'

On black-and-white TV sets back in Brazil and in glorious colour elsewhere, the captain's goal reverberated and resonated around the world. An entire generation fell in love with the beautiful game. Brazil charmed the universe, even if they were far from perfect with a pedestrian goalkeeper, an ordinary backline and an asymmetrical formation.

At the Azteca Stadium, delirious fans, wearing sombreros, poured on to the great green expanse, waving Brazilian flags. It was magic, a human mass in a state of trance. They mobbed the Brazilians and hunted for souvenirs: shirts, shorts, shin pads, boots and even socks. Rivellino fainted and Gérson cried. Pelé was lifted shoulder-high. A big, black sombrero crowned the King.

In the stands, captain Carlos Alberto kissed the glistening Jules Rimet Trophy and lifted it to the sky. The Brazilians had won the World Cup and it was theirs to keep forever. Brazil was, once again, the football nation. 'Brazil 1958 had a very good team and Santos in the 1960s were fantastic, but we played the beautiful game,' said Carlos Alberto.

Chapter XII

Celebration

BRAZIL WAS ECSTATIC. The victory in Mexico had to be feted. For months, weeks and days the Seleção had been at the heart of every conversation, every argument on every doorstep and every street corner. The wonderful final had proven that Brazil was the football nation. The country danced, roared and peacocked. Everyone felt profoundly Brazilian. Even the most ardent left-wing activist – who'd solemnly vowed to never support Brazil – melted when Rivellino equalised in the curtain-raiser against Czechoslovakia. What they'd feared most – in the midst of the political repression and persecution – was euphoria, joy, hope and happiness spreading to every nook and corner of the country. They felt alienated from Brazil, yet the football team had made them happy.

Jubilant, Brazilians lined the streets to see Carlos Alberto and his team in a ticker-tape parade. 'A million supporters in Rio de Janeiro!' *Manchete*, a mainstream magazine not short of superlatives and hyperbole, shouted that it was a party that eclipsed the coronation of Queen Elizabeth II and Neil Armstrong's welcome home.

From Mexico, the Brazilian delegation was first flown to Brasilia for a luncheon and photo-op with President Médici, who seized the moment to champion his regime and bask in the victory. 'In the name of Brazil, thank you very much,' said the general, embracing captain Carlos Alberto. 'You all showed, with a lot of vigour and force, how great our country is. Today is a day of national fraternisation.' Arms wide open and tears streaming down his cheeks, Médici eulogised the team's No. 10: 'You are the great hero, you are the king. You delight our country, Pelé. What great luck that you were born here.' In turn, Pelé cried.

At lunch – a buffet of turkey, duck, roast beef and shrimp – Carlos Alberto, João Havelange and Jerônimo Bastos joined the president's table. Médici was delighted. With the third world title and incredible economic growth, Brazil seemed unstoppable. The military's slogan of '*Ninguem mais segura esta pais*' (Nobody can stop this country now) was becoming reality. Soon, the government would embark on major infrastructure projects, including the construction of the Trans-Amazonian Highway and the Itaipu Dam. Football had contributed its part and the military was planning to take firmer control of the game by launching a proper national championship and constructing bigger and better stadiums than ever before.

Havelange's presidency at the CBD was assured. He, of course, wanted more. In fact, he wanted to run the entire game. His sales pitch to the FIFA electorate would be simple but compelling: a democrat, he represented the 'third world' and would fight for its interests. In the years leading up to the 1974 FIFA presidential elections, Havelange campaigned heavily in Africa, wooing FA presidents with cocktail soirees and promises of banning South Africa's FA because of apartheid. His ultimate selling point was the expansion of the World Cup to a 24-team tournament. The Brazilian was a nefarious football administrator. Pelé was to play a part in mobilising the vote.

The No. 10, however, had plans of his own. Pelé had won it all with the Seleção. He longed for more family time. The endless travelling was exhausting. All the speeches, receptions and official functions, even in the frenzy of victory, as joyous as they were, were overwhelming. He just wanted to sneak away and he was not the only one ...

No. 9 – Tostão

Is Eduardo Gonçalves de Andrade different from Tostão? Can you separate the person from the alter ego? The football player from the doctor? The kid from the septuagenarian? Did Tostão's success and stardom become too much of a burden for Eduardo to carry in later life?

Tostão had been one of those players who longed for some rest amid all the celebrations. Pelé's left-footed attacking partner in the Seleção was priceless to the team. He often played with his back to goal, flicking passes to Pelé and Jairzinho. Everything sped up around him whenever he got possession, his little feet whirring, pinging around his short-range first-time passes. Tostão manipulated the space around him. His intelligence was a menace to opposing defenders. He calculated angles at warp speed and shifted players around him like chess pieces. He pivoted and pirouetted; often, he drifted out to the left.

Tostão wasn't fixated on scoring during the 1970 World Cup. Instead he sought to make himself available at all times, lurking and directing. He embodied one of the great virtues of Zagallo's team – he knew how to play without the ball.

He had a singular kind of understanding with Pelé but knew that he could never match the No. 10:

'When Cruzeiro beat Santos in 66 in the [Taça Brasil] the press was publishing that I was "*o Novo Rei*" (the New King). That was something I thought to be absurd. The press was asking: "How do Pelé and you compare?" I said, "The best that I can do is to think like him, but I just won't be able to execute it, haha!" I could have his logic and reasoning, but I would never have the technique and physical strength to execute it. It was about thinking. Quick thinking in fact is a good quality whatever you do. Being concise, being a minimalist, quickly making decisions without delay.'

Tostão was the team's most sophisticated player. He was brilliant in his own small, decisive patch, drawing out defenders and imagining delicate assists. Yet, Tostão always carried the stigma that he was somewhat underdeveloped for an elite athlete. Even his nickname alluded to his small frame. Eduardo was the little coin, not worth much. Instead he went on to become the brightest player to have ever featured alongside Pelé, anticipating his every move. Armando Nogueira wrote of 'telepathy' between the pair. Tostão called it 'analogue communication'.

For all of Tostão's understanding with Pelé, Eduardo and Edson couldn't have been more different. Edson and Pelé became mythical; the alter ego usurped the person. Tostão's eye injury – which left his fitness for the 1970 World Cup in doubt for the longest of times – ultimately curtailed his career. In 1973 he retired at the age of 26. Tostão was never at home in the hysteria of football milieus.

Intellectual and liberal, he pursued medicine at the Universidade Federal de Minas Gerais, but that didn't bring solace. All his fellow students and professors wanted to talk about was football. His exile from the game would last until 1994 when Tostão returned to the Brazilian mainstream as a TV pundit and columnist. Today, his biweekly columns in *Folha de São Paulo*, a national newspaper, are among the most read and insightful in Brazil.

Eduardo, sitting in his tasteful living room, dressed in a T-shirt from under which a small belly shows, explained:

'It was as if I lived two lives, one of a former athlete – recognised as I am to this day and always trying to be considerate of people; and the other, my personal life, totally separate from my public persona. Football was a diversion. I was a doctor, I worked a lot as a doctor, as a teacher. I stayed away from football. I've always had this concern [to separate Eduardo from Tostão]. I never really liked mixing these things, but it was inevitable. There was no way to separate them.'

In his view, Pelé never suffered from the anguish, the conflict between the man and the myth. There was no loss of identity, the way Tostão and others experienced it. Is Jair separate from Jairzinho? Does Hércules exist without Brito? They've remained captives of their own success. Ultimately, Eduardo couldn't banish football from his life. Instead he's learned to reconcile himself with his alter ego:

'Many have problems, emotional difficulties forming a new life separate from the one they had as athletes. They have a hard time carrying that around. Our Seleção went down in history. Everyone remembered it. Parents and grandparents tell their children and grandchildren. The past is important, it is a living thing used to relate to the modern world. This relationship between the past and the present is important to understand what happens in football today. Yes, the memory is important, but not as something that needs to be relived.'

No. 7 – Jairzinho

It's a February night in 2022 in Leme, a corner of Copacabana beach in the shadow of Sugarloaf Mountain, and Jairzinho is defying the postponement of Carnaval, sambaing the night away at his favourite hangout, Taberna Atlantica. A small band is covering songs by the great composer Cartola, and when it's Jairzinho's turn to take the mic he sings 'Samba Enredo', a 1980s classic. His musical talent is highly questionable but he enraptures the other revellers and demands that Carnaval's inimitable place in the city's calendar is reinstated.

Aged 77, Jairzinho no longer possesses the muscularity and explosiveness of a middleweight boxer he enjoyed during his playing days. Today, he has a beer belly, puffy cheeks and greying hair. He usually wears a tank top adorned with the word 'Fogo', a reference to Botafogo.

With Covid-19 still claiming hundreds of lives a day, sky-high unemployment, poverty and floods in Petropolis, Jairzinho says, 'Brazil has no salvation. In Brazil, nothing ever changes. They want samba and futebol. The population is innocent and enjoys it. But everyone who goes into politics, be it at municipal, state or federal level, it's all about thievery.'

Jairzinho is often loud and argumentative. Everyone at the Taberna knows him and he knows everyone. Yet he carries a resentment from the perception that he never received the recognition that's his due. At the Taberna, he tends to sit at the head of the table. As the evening progresses, he asks his friends, who call him 'Jaja', 'Who here is a champion?' I reply, 'Are you still a champion?' He shouts, 'Who was the best player in 70?' I quip: 'Tostão.'

His friends, Jorge, who thinks Alain Giresse is Polish, and Marcio, a lawyer, don't protest. Jairzinho's attitude is old-school Brazilian: *quem for rei, nunca perde a majestade* – once a world champion, always a world champion. For Jairzinho, however, as time passes, winning the 1970 World Cup seems more a burden than a blessing.

Chapter XIII

The Farewell

WILSON PIAZZA: 'Only God is perfect, but dare I say Pelé was perfect as well?'

Rivellino: 'The King.'

Tostão: 'Pelé had everything.'

Rivellino: 'The greatest player in the world.'

Paulo Henrique: 'Genius.'

Denilson: 'Saviour of the fatherland.'

Antonio Lima: 'Everyone knew Brazil depended on Pelé.'

Paulo Henrique: 'I don't even have the words to describe what Pelé was like.'

Edu: 'He was a father, who taught us how to play.'

Antonio Lima: 'He means everything.'

Marco Antônio: 'He was the best player in the world and, in my mind, he will be until I die.'

Amarildo: 'He was Pelé from the moment he began playing to the moment he retired.'

Paulo Henrique: 'He never said he was going to lose, it was only about winning, do you understand?'

Rivellino: 'Pelé has always been the biggest example in my life. I've never seen him complain about anything.'

Marco Antônio: 'As a kid in Santos, I would go to watch him. He once played the ball off an opponent's leg. I had never seen that.'

Gérson: 'His thinking was always ahead of you.'

Marco Antônio: 'God gave him everything.'

Tostão: 'It was as if he was a computer – he calculated all movements of the opponents and the ball.'

Rivellino: 'There are certain athletes who should be eternal.'

Marco Antônio: 'I could die here and now, but I played alongside Pelé and that remains my salvation.'

Rivellino: 'Thank God, he was born Brazilian.'

Rivellino: 'And, I think, there won't be anyone like him.'

* * *

Those who played and trained with Pelé feel privileged. They performed on pitches lit up by his radiance and dwelt in a 'Pelé universe'. He was the synthesis of all talent. The lodestar of Santos. The talisman and top scorer of the Seleção. Triple world champion. Football's first global superstar. Brazil's ambassador. Black icon.

With his short haircut, oval face, bright eyes and impressive physique, Pelé seemed ageless. Yet, on a sunny afternoon in July 1971, when Brazil took on Yugoslavia, the Maracanã clamoured for him one last time. The week before, São Paulo had feted him with a crown and a sceptre after a 1-1 draw against Austria. Rio left such hyperbole aside. From the stands, the fans implored him to stay, but the No. 10 was adamant: this would be his farewell match in the Brazil shirt. Amid the reverence and festivities, Pelé's mind was drifting back to his father, Dondinho, who gave his son a simple piece of advice: 'Quit, not when you are asked to retire; quit at the top.' Pelé did just that.

A skilled player but with a career curtailed by injury, Dondinho internalised the trauma of his career before passing his dreams on to his son. Pelé always wanted to emulate his father, much to the dismay of his mother, Dona Celeste, who viewed football as an unstable profession, one that brought Dondinho too much sadness and suffering. Why should her son experience the same torment? How would he provide for his family? At the age of 13, Pelé contributed to his parents' household as a shoe-shiner and as a vendor of stolen peanuts ... to his neighbourhood club.

His parents shaped him: from his father, he got the drive to train harder, run faster, play better and think smarter; from his mother, the fear of financial insecurity. Pride and fear equally moved the young Pelé. They, in part, made him outgrow Zizinho, his idol and Brazil's 1950 midfield metronome.

At a young age Pelé became synonymous with the World Cup. He was the hero, who rose, fell and triumphed in a classic play in three acts. By 1970 he was no longer the skinny teenager of Sweden 1958, but a stocky, cerebral player. Mature and calculated, his game was pragmatic and frugal. Roberto Miranda said, 'He no longer had that velocity, intensity, he didn't have that anymore. He played with the name that he had acquired in the previous World Cups.'

The world never saw Pelé at his best. TV simply wasn't around in the early 1960s. Even Jairzinho wonders how the spell of Pelé, an abstract genius to the modern mind, has persisted. He asked, 'How is this extraordinary myth, that of a player considered the athlete of the century, being kept alive so strongly? It makes you reflect and think a lot, things look unreal.'

'Those who didn't follow Pelé from the start have a distorted view – that Pelé had his peak at the World Cup in 1970,' explained Tostão, who watched Pelé as a teenager. 'What happened with Pelé was the following: from 1957 until 1964, more or less, that was his pinnacle, because he was quick. He went to the [1970] World Cup, consecrated. There was a championship in 1959 in which he scored two, three goals in every game, each one more spectacular than the last. He was so spectacular in a short period of time.'

Tostão pointed out that Pelé, in reality, hardly trained. From one match to the next, he barely had time to recover. He said, 'Santos played too much. Everyone, the whole world, wanted to see Santos play. He never trained, he never prepared. From the age of 16 he followed that rhythm. It's absurd.'

Gérson said, 'Watching a rested Pelé is one thing, watching Pelé on a crazy tour is something else.'

'He never had specific fitness coaching. He was a natural phenomenon. He had speed, acceleration and physical capacity, all without preparation,' added Tostão.

This Pelé danced through defences with the ball glued to his feet: the slick and sinuous movement of his goal against Mexico at the 1962 World Cup; the pace, poise and balance of his wonder strike against Benfica that same year in the Intercontinental Cup; exploits the leaner Pelé of 1958 and the bulkier Pelé of 1970 wouldn't have accomplished. He embodied, for the first time perhaps, the concept of a modern-day player, of today's super athletes. His football was a study in precision at an inconceivable pace.

Even in Mexico, where he often conserved his energy, he remained unstoppable. Pelé's genius was indestructible. His audacious shot from the halfway line against Czechoslovakia was a simple message to his detractors: Pelé was still the best. He'd fooled his opponents. They thought they could contain a slower and older Pelé. But nobody could. In a way, Moore came closest, but to no avail. Did Alan Ball mark Pelé well? Perhaps. Ball's effort was commendable but he was guilty of the cardinal sin: letting Pelé out of his sight for a split second.

'He saved himself to keep going,' said Robert Miranda. 'He slowed down and then went again.'

'He could no longer ignite, but he still worried three opponents,' said Marco Antônio.

His athleticism prevailed because his mind raced faster. His brain matched his feet.

'He saw things differently, right?' explained Gérson. 'He noticed things before others did, that's why you had to be … You weren't going to compare yourself to him, so you had to always be on his tail, watching the play, but knowing where he was. Suddenly, he'd move. The players at the back, who set up the play, in particular for Pelé, had to have all their senses switched on because, otherwise, the moment would pass. And then came the complaint: "Are you sleeping back there?" For my set-piece pass against [Czechoslovakia] to Pelé, which he controlled on his chest and scored from, I was watching him from on our half. I noticed that he was beginning to move to the outside of the defender. I did the same thing for the third goal against Italy, he headed the ball to Jairzinho.'

'I learned [from Pelé] to have a different view of the game – to observe my team-mates and the opponents before I received the ball,' said Clodoaldo.

Brazilian teams were always a good mix of artists and athletes, of the cerebral and vigorous. In 1958

Dadá and Garrincha were the virtuosos, Zagallo and Vava industrious. In 1970 Jairzinho was a sheer force of nature – a 'bull' according to Tostão – whereas Gérson, Rivellino and Tostão were the aesthetes. Pelé conflated the two characteristics the best. It's what set him apart in a team of stars: he was both the supreme athlete and supreme artist.

'Well, Pelé never ceased to surprise with new moves,' said Carlos Alberto. 'His halfway line attempt against Czechoslovakia was audacious. It was the first time a player had tried to do that; today everybody does it. For 12 years I played with Pelé at Santos and then at the Cosmos. Every game he played, Pelé could surprise. Those two moments against Uruguay were again unique. Pelé tried to do something that hadn't been done before. In every game, he improvised, a hallmark of great Brazilian players.'

In a tribute for magazine *Eight by Eight*, journalist and book editor David Hirshey wrote of Pelé's most illuminative moment in the semi-final:

'... he stretched the boundaries of logic as far as humanly possible. Racing toward a seeing-eye through ball from the diminutive centre-forward Tostão that put him one on one with Uruguay's standout goalkeeper Ladislao Mazurkiwiecz, Pelé appeared to have two choices: 1) chip the hard-charging keeper while running at full tilt; 2) drop a shoulder and dribble around him. He had a fraction to make those calculations ... Pelé dismissed the two expected options, even though either manoeuvre would doubtlessly have resulted in an easy goal. But where's the fun in that? In that instant, he had the audacity to reach for soccer perfection and rip a hole in the space-time continuum ... His off-balance shot trickled past the far post by a centimetre, making it the greatest goal never scored in World Cup history.'

Jairzinho said, 'Pelé let the ball pass and, in a capricious way, that thing that makes football, it was that marvellous move – moments like that, the unmissable, unforgettable ones – that lived on the longest in our minds, in the minds of fans, even more so than a real goal, do you understand?'

'It's funny, you know?' chuckled Dadá, observing that 'if it had been Jairzinho or Tostão, no one would comment on the attempts that didn't go in'.

By 1970, and because of 1970, Nelson Rodrigues's prophecy that Pelé belonged 'more to the mythology of football than to football itself' had come true. Pelé had been crowned the greatest player of all time and Brazil the happy free-wheeling masters of the game. Rodrigues had been the first to call Pelé the King and to the great playwright, who had little knowledge of the actual game, he was precisely that. But for those who played alongside Pelé, he was everything.

'We are with the King, we are with God,' Piazza remembered, lost in thought.

God and ten mortals formed the Brazilian team. That the No. 10 was a master at wrapping his arms around opponents and conning the referees is conveniently forgotten. Tostão went as far as to say: 'He simulated at times, but it didn't stand out.' Even his fouling is praised, notably elbowing Uruguay's Fontes as a reprisal in the semi-final. Piazza explains that Pelé 'even knew how to go in hard, how to kick the shit out of someone'.

Tostão added, 'That aggression was part of his talent, because, above all, one of Pelé's greatest qualities was that when things were difficult, he was more aggressive. He had that desire, he wanted to turn things around. At times he shoved the defender. He used his body, his arms. [He was] aggressive and malicious. He wanted to win. He was a beast. He was not a soft player, to the contrary.'

'He always said, "We must win, we will win!"' added Rivellino.

Pelé's benediction has no boundaries. They revered him when he closed his eyes on the bus or in the dressing room before a match to get in 'his mood', his mindset to allow him to outclass opponents and to keep on winning. Paulo Henrique recalled, 'He would lie down, relaxing, with a towel. He was meditating for about five minutes. He had to do that to know what he had to do. He had to concentrate because for him everything was football, football, football. And he would lie there and be quiet. No one would mess with him. It was only him, only he did it. It was his.'

'Pelé showed himself to be humble,' added Roberto Miranda, sarcastically.

His meditation was also part of his cunning. He understood how to awe those around him, how to imbue himself with that veneration. In Mexico, Pelé was focused on his own objectives, as he'd always been. This was to be his last World Cup. It was his final chance to ascend the pantheon of the gods. 'We knew that he was *O Rei* (the King), but to us he seemed just another guy,' said Edu.

With his third World Cup victory, Pelé transcended the game. He'd become an icon. Brazilians adored Garrincha, with whom they could identify themselves. Life was harsh on him, he didn't belong to the establishment and his success was restricted to the pitch. But Pelé belonged to a different category altogether. He enacted Brazil's ultimate collective fantasy: victory rendered the country important. Pelé represented a successful Brazil, a nation that taught the world.

For the government, he was a useful propaganda tool, an emblem of a united, buoyant nation on the march. A soldier in 1959, Pelé was alien to politics. He neither criticised the military dictatorship nor questioned the absence of democracy in Brazil. He was happy to receive the medal of the Order of Rio Branco alongside high-ranking members of the Serviço

Nacional de Informaçao, the dictatorship's secret service, and to fete the 1970 world title with General Médici at the Planalto. Did that fraternisation render Pelé an ally of the regime? This was a question that, as time passed by, was never truly answered. Pelé always remained vague about his own attitude during the military dictatorship.

For many football fans Pelé was the greatest ever. They moulded him – the man and the hero – to their own needs and likings. Kings, prime ministers, supermodels, rock stars, groupies, football officials, agents, broadcasters, journalists and hangers-on, everyone wanted a piece of Pelé. A football persona isn't meant to hold such significance but Pelé lent himself to it. His aura unmatchable, he responded with friendliness and an infectious smile. Edson loved being Pelé, the superhero. He loved being the King.

Images captured of Pelé during his prime, and decades thereafter, reveal a life that must have been desperately claustrophobic. Amid all the euphoria and hysteria, Pelé always had to oblige the circus. 'People wanted to touch him, take pictures, in short, see if Pelé was really human,' said Clodoaldo. 'On tour with Santos, he was almost seen as an extra-terrestrial.'

For mortals this would have been a life of incomparable solitude, hidden in plain sight, but not to Pelé. He always believed that he was the best, the greatest. Sitting at the table of his Santos lodgings, listening to the radio, Pelé, 17, wasn't shocked to be called up for the 1958 World Cup and to be named alongside greats like Didi, Djalma Santos and Nilton Santos. No, he'd expected it. Early on he embraced what he perceived to be his destiny.

In an interview with *Jornal dos Sports* during the week leading up to his 1971 farewell match, he trotted out a line that he'd repeat over the years – Pelé was to become immortal. He was discussing his silly dream of winning an Oscar, wrapping up the final scenes of *A Marcha*, a movie in which he, implausibly, played Chico Bondade, the leader of an abolitionist movement. The interview's context was different, but the underlying idea was the same – Pelé would never die. He already referred to himself in the third person. Edson had vanished, usurped by Pelé.

Those close to him, Antonio Lima, Edu, Pepe and Mengálvio, the old Santos guard, who still frequent his seaside house in Guaruja for long and joyful lunches or *café com leite*, argue that Edson is still around, you can be with the man who has put up with Pelé his entire life. Edu said, 'Pelé wouldn't be Pelé without Edson. Pelé stood out as Edson did as well, with his qualities and possibilities, like a normal person. He has humility and respect for family and friends. He receives us very well. His joy and happiness when he sees us is something fantastic, spectacular. We bring him some happiness as well.'

'He joked with us: "If you think you will get rid of me, you can think again!"' recalled Lima.

Back in 1971, against Yugoslavia, Brazilians simply wanted their football star to not retire. He wasn't yet in the autumn of his career. He could still defy what convention dictated one could do with a ball. But Pelé, who redefined the game as well as the image of his nation, ignored the calls and cries. The King was abdicating.

No. 18 – Caju

Paulo Cézar Caju had the world at his feet. Two-footed and obscenely talented, he played superbly against both England and Romania in the group stages of the 1970 World Cup. He tormented right-sided full-backs Tommy Wright and Lajos Sătmăreanu. Aged 21, he was considered Pelé's heir, but his career, despite success with both Botafogo and Brazil, never attained the heights his talent promised.

Today, Caju, identifiable through his walrus moustache, writes columns for Brazilian media. His world view, at least when it comes to football, is reductive: 'In the past everything was marvellous, today it's all shit.' He is impatient with the low skill level of the contemporary game and the invasion of the technocrats. His opinions divide, they always have. Some think Caju is an arrogant, contrarian know-it-all.

When he was still a player he was idiosyncratic, opinionated and progressive. A bohemian, Caju loved fast cars and bell-bottom jeans. He hung out with Marilena Dabus, Brazil's first female football journalist, and Canal 100's Carlos Niemeyer. Caju liked to party at Ipanema's flashiest clubs. After his career he indulged the jet-set life too much at cocaine and champagne-laden parties in France.

He even had to sell his World Cup medal to sustain his addiction.

But his behaviour, unheard of in the 1970s for a man of colour, rattled the Brazilian establishment: he'd acquired all the privileges of the white ruling class – and Caju couldn't care less. In fact, he felt it was his damned right. Caju wasn't the obedient black player of the time, who entertained white supporters in the stands before returning home to the favela, the role that Pelé accepted and acquiesced to, that of the submissive, black player who knew his place.

Reading about the Black Panthers in the United States, Caju embraced the Black Power movement. Defending the black cause, he was deemed a rebel. In 1966 Pelé declined an invitation to be feted by the black community in Harlem. A *garoto propaganda* (poster boy), he was never going to upset the established order. Perhaps, after the 1970 World Cup, Pelé, exploiting his brand, became a victim of racism himself: a part of the press painted him as a greedy mercenary, a black man unfit to be a businessman.

Even so, Pelé always shied away from a more combative stance on race in Brazil, something Caju laments profoundly. His complaint then is simple: when did Pelé ever defend the black cause?

Chapter XIV

The Decline

AT THE 1974 World Cup in Germany, Pelé was back. Just not as the establishment had imagined it – the military and Havelange had asked him to reconsider his retirement but Pelé was resolute. On the sidelines, often in a suit, he was something of a rock star. He promoted Pepsi-Cola, dispensed pleasantries, shook hands and analysed the tournament. One of his insights proved to be prophetic: the Netherlands were among the favourites. Unfortunately, Zagallo and his team didn't heed Pelé's words.

So it was on 3 July, in Dortmund, that the Brazilians didn't quite understand what hit them. They'd never seen anything like it, the movement on and off the ball – so entirely natural and spontaneous. The white shirts whizzed easily and gracefully past the blue ones – Brazil were the away team. Technically impeccable, the Dutch sparkled with energy and imagination. The pressing was maniacal: the triangulations, the finesse. It was all urbane, distinguished and, in a way, extravagant.

On closer inspection, the Dutch didn't really look like athletes. You noticed the sideburns of Willem van Hanegem, the unkempt, long hair of Johan Neeskens and the nonchalance of Johan Cruyff. They rather looked like the hippies who'd flourished in the Netherlands of the late 1960s, but their soft appearance belied their excellence. The Brazilians should have known this. In club football the Dutch had already shown that they were a new force.

Two months before Brazil's triumph in Mexico, Feyenoord's 2-1 win in the European Cup Final against Celtic heralded the glorious intricacies of the Dutch game and its sophisticated football system. The Rotterdam outfit was the first Dutch club to triumph in a continental competition. A reader of the Scottish magazine *Celtic View* poignantly wrote after the match that 'Feyenoord's maddening, clinical, almost military precision of successive forward, diagonal, backward and triangular traceries was more in keeping with a geometrical exercise than a cup final. Irritating to watch to a degree – but it got them the European Cup.'

Soon, Ajax Amsterdam dominated the continental club game. Rinus Michels, *Totaalvoetbal*, 4-3-3 and the balletic Cruyff swept the game and steered it towards more holistic philosophies. Inspired by the Netherlands' cultural liberalisation, the Dutch reframed the essence of the game: football was about exploiting space. In *Brilliant Orange*, David Winner identifies spatial creativity, architecture and planning as cornerstones of the Dutch concept of the game.

Dutch club football mirrored the sophistication of Dutch society. The national team, on the other hand, didn't immediately catch on. Hence, the Brazilians could be somewhat forgiven for their ignorance. When the Dutch didn't participate in the 1972 *Taça Independencia*, Brazilian magazine *Placar* wrote that it didn't matter much – the audience wasn't missing out on anything. The implication was not to be misunderstood: the Netherlands weren't very relevant – or perhaps, the journalists at the famous magazine weren't well informed.

True, the Netherlands didn't have much of a track record in the international game. In fact, they weren't much better than Luxembourg. In the 1960s they'd still been playing in the W-M formation, but by 1974, returning to the World Cup for the first time since 1938, Oranje, with its core of Ajax and Feyenoord players, was a different team altogether. They relegated Uruguay, Bulgaria, Argentina and East Germany to bystanders. In a goalless draw, only Sweden offered a pocket of resistance.

The Dutch were playing the football of the future. In and out of possession, they elevated the game to new levels, prompting coach Michels to comment that

Cruyff was good on the ball and very good off it. He built his team around a solid defence, one of Zagallo's dogmas as well. Dutch newspaper *Handelsblad* was lyrical: 'Oranje is too good for this world. They play a *Totaalvoetbal* that others cannot match.'

The Brazilians worked tirelessly to compensate for their comparative lack of star power by being overly physical. From the 1970 squad: Emerson Leão, Marco Antônio, Zé Maria, Wilson Piazza, Paulo Cézar Caju, Rivellino, Edu and Jairzinho remained. Only Rivellino and Jairzinho were guaranteed starters. Luís Pereira and Marinho Peres formed the core of a hardened defence – an improvement from the Piazza–Brito pair. Further upfield, Rivellino, de facto playmaker, and Caju were tenacious, but not imposing enough in the opponent's half. Even Rivellino's trademark free kicks were predictable. His role was often clipped by the ball-hogging Jairzinho at centre-forward, who held off players close to the penalty box with his arms, in order to provoke free kicks. On the right wing, Valdomiro was hardly convincing.

This was still a talented squad, but one with limitations. And as such Brazil tried to minimise the strengths of the opponents rather than maximise their own. 'We currently have strong defenders and a dogma in football theory is that you should use your strongest weapons,' said Zagallo. 'That's why we play more defensively than ever.'

'Our playing style is tailored to prevent conceding,' said Luís Pereira, chain-smoking filter cigarettes at the team hotel in Germany.

'Luís Pereira and Marinho Chagas were the only defenders to move up the field,' said Zé Maria, a reserve during the 1970 World Cup.

'It doesn't allow for a lot of attacking,' added left-back Marinho Chagas. 'When I venture forward, no one covers and that was almost fatal against Argentina.'

Each and every match was telling of how defence had come to define Brazil. The once bright and brisk world champions struggled their way through the tournament, escaping embarrassment in goalless draws against both Yugoslavia and Scotland. The 3-0 victory in the final group game against Zaire, debutants and whipping boys, was fortuitous: goalkeeper Kazadi Mwamba blundered, conceding the third goal. Brazil progressed at the expense of Scotland. 'Valdomiro's goal was a very lucky goal,' said Zé Maria. 'The ball went in because it was Brazil playing. If it had been another team, perhaps it wouldn't have gone in.'

In the knockout group, they edged past East Germany and Argentina. The Seleção were economic, not shy of roughing up opponents with professional fouls and cynical tackles. They left the initiative, space and advantage to their opponents. Brazil adopted a counter-attacking style with the anomaly of not really counter-attacking: in transition, their ball circulation was simply too slow. Their newly adopted style was jarring and shocking: how did the team metamorphose from the immortal XI of 1970 to the cynical side of the 1974 World Cup? Brazil were the most criticised team of the tournament, their realism and pragmatism sparked contempt.

On the eve of the all-deciding encounter with the Netherlands – Brazil needed a win to reach the final – Zagallo claimed that Brazil could do better than they'd shown so far. True, in 450 minutes of play Brazil had conceded just one goal and they had no intention to destroy the game against the Netherlands from the onset.

The Seleção were combative with long passes forward so as to exploit Oranje's high defensive line, only to be flagged offside as often. Before the break, Paulo Cézar Caju and Jairzinho came agonisingly close to the opening goal but the match had become far too brutal, far too soon. Zé Maria characterised the encounter 'as the most aggressive in the competition' and 'disputed with virility'. Marinho floored Neeskens. It wasn't just the Brazilians who were vicious. Van Hanegem, Wim Suurbier and Johnny Rep produced some flying tackles of their own.

Neeskens was frequently to be found furthest forward. He almost played as a striker, allowing the entire team to move upfield as a compact unit. Out of possession, Oranje harried their opponents, who were constantly on the back foot, struggling to understand, let alone react, to the ingenious ball rotation and recuperation of the Dutch.

Wave after wave, Dutch attacks crashed over the Brazilians and in the 50th minute the two Johans combined for the opening goal; Neeskens arrived before Pereira to lift the ball over goalkeeper Leão with a single touch from Cruyff's assist. Brazil were being overwhelmed. The Netherlands' second goal was simple but brilliant. Rob Rensenbrink's pass split open the Brazilian defence and Cruyff volleyed home from Ruud Krol's left-wing cross, drawing Zé Maria and Marinho Peres hopelessly out of position.

Everything happened so quickly and was perfectly executed. The Dutch seemed to forget about tactics, philosophies and even systems. They interchanged or, as Marinho Peres had noted himself, 'They run around through each other so much that you can't distinguish strikers from defenders.'

Zé Maria should have marked Rensenbrink, but he didn't see it as such. He said, 'In truth, there was no direct opponent. Everyone just floated around. They were always interchanging, occupying space.'

'They should have scored six or seven,' recalled Marco Antônio, who didn't play a single minute in that World Cup. 'I thought the field was small, as if reduced, and they had that thing where everyone moved upfield at the same time, leaving the opponent offside. Cruyff was just fooling around, joking. What a beautiful thing, the most beautiful thing in the world was to watch Holland in 74.'

The Brazilians retaliated with more violence. Their ruthlessness was pathetic and an expression of powerlessness. In the 84th minute Pereira mowed down Neeskens and was sent off. Although a fine sweeper and central defender, Pereira's rough display exposed an unhappy side that killed the game's spirit. The Seleção found no joy in defending their world title and were playing dated gridiron football.

Pereira was the first-ever Brazilian to receive a material red card at a World Cup. From the touchline, he provoked the Dutch supporters and became the symbol of a transgressive team. 'I only showed the Dutch fans with my fingers that we had won the World Cup three times,' lamented Pereira, who works for Atlético Madrid today.

A man down, Zagallo reshuffled his team. Stripped of the captain's armband against Argentina, Piazza was reluctant to come on as a substitute, in the cold, dying minutes of the match. He seemed to rebel against the inevitable.

Great teams shouldn't decline in this manner. The 1974 World Cup was particularly difficult for Brazil: they had to defend their title in Europe and with a decimated team. Pelé, Tostão and Gérson had retired from the Seleção and both Carlos Alberto and Clodoaldo were injured. 'Do you have an idea of what it is to be without Gérson?' questioned Jairzinho. 'No! Do you have an idea of what it is to be without Carlos Alberto? Damned, Zagallo managed the group according to the quality of the players at his disposal.'

'He made a team according to his understanding and with the human resources at his disposal,' added Zé Maria. 'A strong, deep-lying defence, with a lot of marking. A deep-lying winger. And Jairzinho, who had to pivot.'

'You can't live without Pelé,' said Rivellino. 'Certain athletes should be eternal. But it's no use thinking, "Oh, Pelé should be here! Pelé, Pelé, Pelé."'

'The retirements left the Seleção unstructured,' explained Tostão. 'It was a different team and that is what happens to most after such an achievement – the disintegration. It's why Brazil are the only team to have been consecutive world champions [Italy won the tournament in 1934 and 1938].'

Brazil had wanted to repeat the success formula of Mexico, with a lengthy, protracted preparation to fine-tune team tactics and strengthen the players' physique. In 1974 they spent weeks together, first at home, drawing goalless against Austria and Greece, and then acclimatising for a month in Germany's Black Forest. Brazil's team hotel became a fortress because of the tragedy at the 1972 Olympic Games. 'One night, we were sleeping and there was supposedly a bomb in the hotel,' recalled Valdomiro. 'Everyone ran out and there were guards and German soldiers taking care of things. Armed soldiers and tanks in front of the hotel entrance. Everything was sealed off.'

Inside the hotel, the old fissures festered between players from Rio de Janeiro and São Paulo. With little kinship in the squad, the atmosphere was oppressive and bad. 'It was Paulistas against Cariocas,' said Zé Maria. 'There were insinuations going around in the group and you'd think. "Could it be? Damn, is this guy against me?" I'd be your reserve, but I wasn't rooting for you. There was no mutual respect. My reserve was Nelinho, a very good friend, and I supported him, I can say that wholeheartedly. A lot of players didn't feel that way. Like Marinho Chagas and Marco Antônio: Marco Antônio wanted to play.'

'Brazil was not prepared,' said Piazza. In his office, he examines an informal team photo that, in his view, captures the Zeitgeist. What he sees still fills him with regret.

There was extravagance and, perhaps, excess. The Brazilians were stars and wanted to enjoy their status. Afro hairstyles and trendy garments were a must. Paulo Cézar Caju personified the new age of the liberated, self-conscious player. He loved fast cars and the in-crowd. He dressed accordingly. Above all, Paulo Cézar Caju was a black star who upset the establishment by demanding and acquiring all the privileges and prerogatives of the white elite. He wanted to indulge in the good life and, rightly, believed he'd earned the right to do so. He partied at Hippopotamus, Ipanema's famed nightclub.

'Oh, it was about fashion, bell-bottom jeans, cornrows and The Beatles,' explained Piazza. 'Paulo Cézar Caju would walk up and say, "Look at this fool over here, look at his pants. They are out of fashion!" He was mocking me. Yes? I was always one of the "you do what you want, but I don't!" And that was missing in 1974, my personality and a better-formed conscience of not getting carried away.'

'You have to drop your vanity at a World Cup,' added Zé Maria.

Piazza himself wasn't without fault. A year earlier, as captain on a European tour, he'd led a press boycott during the so-called 'demonstrations of Glasgow'. It was an unprecedented move in retaliation for negative press coverage and what the players perceived to be intrusions into their private lives.

Piazza recalled: 'I was married, but in Sweden ... Tomorrow will be a day off, I've got a girl, a Swedish girl, and I am going to the restaurant [with her], have a drink with her, then head off to the motel. It's cultural. Even as a matter of physiological need, because otherwise it's just training, just playing ... You're young, you have all that strength and you need to release it.'

'Piazza was crucified [for the boycott],' said Zé Maria. 'He didn't want it. It wasn't good for the Seleção. We ended up prejudiced.'

By the time of the match against the Netherlands, Zagallo had dropped Piazza, who'd played a tournament of imprecision and melancholy. Rivellino, in the No. 10 shirt, was a shadow of himself: Yugoslavian midfielders Branko Oblak and Jovan Aćimović marked him out of the opening match. He didn't even impress against Zaire. Paulo Cézsar Caju failed to ignite in a tournament that should have been his. Jairzinho had lost his greatest trademark, speed. Both Caju and Jairzinho were distracted by imminent transfers to France.

Brazil were a lethargic and often querulous team. In the face of criticism, Zagallo accused the press of misrepresenting the truth. In his view, Brazil didn't play too defensively. His demeanour was that of a man happy with Brazil's progress. 'He didn't hit his fist on the table,' said Zé Maria. 'He was satisfied with what was happening.'

Brazil's coach didn't abandon his 4-3-3. It was the cornerstone of his success and three world titles won at the age of 26, 30 and 38. Zagallo had little incentive to question the formula that had always brought him success. It was the curse of achieving glory all too early. As a media analyst at the 1998 World Cup in France, Tostão pointed out that Zagallo was still using the training methods of the 1970s.

'We didn't deserve to win,' reflected Piazza. 'You have to do a *mea culpa*.'

'It wasn't a decline,' Jairzinho told me. 'You can't always win. The Netherlands were already more modern, but they didn't go on to become world champions. It was false modernity. They lost against the German machine. They shuddered against the Germans. They didn't win anything. It was a negative revolution. Holland were champions of nothing. They will never instigate another revolution like that. What, Holland? You, Brazilians, have such ideas. A team is not good when it doesn't win a championship. *Pra caramba*.'

In the days after the elimination, *Jornal do Brasil* concluded, somewhat more objectively than Jairzinho all these many years later, that 'the defending champions got a masterclass in modern football. We didn't know much about Cruyff. Now we will never forget him.'

Cruyff and the best team to never win the World Cup ended Brazil's golden era. Didi. Garrincha. Pelé. Jairzinho. Gérson. Tostão. Carlos Alberto's strike, the most exhilarating goal in the history of the World Cup. Three global crowns. All of that belonged to the past, to a yesteryear that had charmed and captivated and that came to define Brazil to the rest of the world.

Brazil were struggling to enter the new world. Their football was more rigid and introspective and, in years to come, they'd exhibit other, more mundane qualities with mounting confidence. Yet, at the club level, some domestic coaches picked up on the Dutch revolution. Olaria played a high line in the Rio State Championship, a strategy that Coutinho's Flamengo scuppered with overlapping.

A technocrat of sophistication, Coutinho led Brazil at the 1978 World Cup in Argentina, where he tried to imitate the Netherlands. That was almost contradictory: his technocratic approach advanced a style that devalued self-expression and favoured a physical, European style. Brazilian football's golden age was over. The new direction was clear: Brazil wanted to win in a different way and replaced artists with bulky athletes.

Tostão reflected: 'The Seleção of 1970 was revolutionary, enchanting the entire world, but she was the beginning of the fall. The development of the physical and scientific aspects was beginning to be valued in an absurd way with a preference for coaches from the physical education class, like Parreira. That prompted a drop in quality for a period. Parreira and Coutinho were the great ambassadors of that change in the game.'

The Brazilians were never to recapture that 1970s magic and reach the heights of their golden epoch. That win became a strangely haunting image. Inadvertently, Brazil's greatest victory led to the decay of everything they'd stood for: the skill, the individualism, the beauty and the belief that football was a sport to be enjoyed, and a game to stir the soul.

Epilogue

The Greatest Team of All Time

THE BRAZIL of 1970 were the greatest team of all time. After all, more than 50 years later, they still are a universal reference. Brazil's victory mattered.

The Brazilians seized their moment in history – the arrival of worldwide television, so imaginatively launched for all of mankind with Neil Armstrong's steps on the moon in 1969 and Carlos Alberto's strike against Italy, compelling Jonathon Wilson to write in *Inverting the Pyramid* that Brazil's victory came 'to be regarded as a greater endeavour … as though to play football of that majesty were somehow a victory for all of humanity'.

Mexico 1970 was the first non-European World Cup transmitted live, beamed to a global audience, much more so than the 1966 World Cup in England in fuzzy black-and-white images. The light in Mexico was incredibly intense, Brazil's canary yellow, shimmering gold shirts with cobalt blue shorts were perfect for the new medium. TV turned the World Cup into a unique and unrivalled cultural phenomenon. The sport, for the first time, had a global community.

Under the midday Mexican sun and in brutal conditions, the game was often languid with so much space and little closing down, but the Brazilians delivered in, arguably, the best World Cup ever. They swept past the opposition, scoring 12 of their 19 goals in the second half, a testimony to their physical fitness, fostered over months of preparation and backed up by science.

Brazil were irresistible in the tournament's showpiece match. They completely outclassed Italy, even tactically, dispatching the stereotype of happy, samba-dancing football players assembled from a beach. Over decades of romantic reverie, that myth, though, has endured – the image of Brazil playing loosely with improvisation and spontaneity, obliging beauty and nothing else.

Instead, they fostered a greater and wider understanding of football, in particular the balance between the individual and the team, part of the game's continuum. As Johan Cruyff and Franz Beckenbauer proved at the 1974 World Cup, individualism wasn't finished yet, but football was moving towards holistic systems, towards homogenisation.

In the new era, club football overtook the international game. In 1970 Brazil were the best of elite football, but only four years later Ajax Amsterdam and Bayern Munich had overtaken their respective national teams, forming the backbone and creative forces behind the Netherlands and West Germany.

The Netherlands team of 1974 belong to a vast category of nearly men – akin to Hungary 1954 and Brazil 1982. Their drama needs little elaboration: they were sexy and cool, often revolutionary, but never achieved the ultimate. Spain did so at the 2010 World Cup and reshaped the modern game in a marvellous spectacle of passing, positioning and pressing. All of these teams can claim greatness.

As can Brazil's side from 1958, the first Seleção to win the global crown. With Djalma Santos, Bellini, Orlando and Nilton Santos in the backline and luminaries Didi and Garrincha further upfield, they were superior man for man to Brazil 1970, a more modern and compact team. It's a point that Gérson, Tostão, Rivellino and others are all too happy to concede. In fact, they adore their predecessors from the Sweden World Cup. It was the team of their childhood. But Brazil 1970 is the team of our childhood.

Appendix

Road to the Azteca

1969 World Cup Qualifiers
6 August, Colombia vs Brazil 0-2
10 August, Venezuela vs Brazil 0-5
17 August, Paraguay vs Brazil 0-3
21 August, Brazil vs Colombia 6-2
24 August, Brazil vs Venezuela 6-0
31 August, Brazil vs Paraguay 1-0

1970 World Cup finals
Group stage
Czechoslovakia vs Brazil 1-4
3 June 1970, Estadio Jalisco, Guadalajara
Referee: Ramón R. Barreto (Uruguay)
Brazil: Félix; Carlos Alberto, Brito, Piazza, Everaldo; Clodoaldo, Gérson (Paulo Cézar Caju 62), Rivellino; Jairzinho, Tostão, Pelé
Manager: Mário Lobo Zagallo

Czechoslovakia: Ivo Viktor, Karol Dobiaš, Václav Migas, Vladimir Hagara, Alexander Horváth, Ladislav Kuna, František Veselý (Bohumil Veselý 75), Ladislav

Petráš, Jozef Adamec, Karol Jokl, Ivan Hrdlička (Andrej Kvašňák 45)
Manager: Jozef Marko
Scorers: Ladislav Petráš (11), Rivellino (24), Pelé (59), Jairzinho (61, 83)

England vs Brazil 0-1
7 June 1970, Estadio Jalisco, Guadalajara
Referee: Abraham Klein (Israel)
Brazil: Félix; Carlos Alberto, Brito, Wilson Piazza, Everaldo; Clodoaldo, Rivellino, Paulo Cézar Caju; Jairzinho, Tostão (Roberto Miranda 68), Pelé
Manager: Mário Lobo Zagallo

England: Gordon Banks, Terry Cooper, Brian Labone, Tommy Wright, Bobby Moore, Alan Mullery, Alan Ball, Bobby Charlton (Colin Bell 64), Martin Peters, Geoff Hurst, Francis Lee (Astle 64)
Manager: Alf Ramsey
Scorers: Jairzinho (59)

Romania vs Brazil 2-3
10 June 1970, Estadio Jalisco, Guadalajara
Referee: Ferdinand Marschall (Austria)
Brazil: Félix; Carlos Alberto, Brito, Wilson Piazza, Everaldo (Marco Antônio 56); Fontana, Clodoaldo (Edu 73), Paulo Cézar Caju; Jairzinho, Tostão, Pelé
Manager: Mário Lobo Zagallo

Romania: Stere Adamache (Necula Răducanu 28), Ludovic Sătmăreanu, Nicolae Lupescu, Cornel Dinu, Mihai Mocanu, Ion Dumitru, Radu Nunweiler, Emerich Dembrovschi, Alexandru Neagu, Florea Dumitrache (Gheorghe Tătaru 71), Mircea Lucescu

Manager: Angelo Niculescu
Scorers: Pelé (19, 67), Jairzinho (22), Dumitrache (34), Dembrovschi (84)

Quarter-Finals
Brazil vs Peru 4-2
14 June 1970, Estadio Jalisco, Guadalajara
Referee: Vital Loraux (Belgium)
Brazil: Félix; Carlos Alberto, Brito, Wilson Piazza, Marco Antônio; Clodoaldo, Gérson (Paulo Cézar Caju 67), Rivellino; Jairzinho (Roberto Miranda 80), Tostão, Pelé
Manager: Mário Lobo Zagallo

Peru: Luis Rubiños, Eloy Campos, Héctor Chumpitaz, Nicolás Fuentes, José Fernández, Ramón Mifflin, Roberto Challe, Julio Baylón (Hugo Sotil 53), Pedro León (Eladio Reyes 61), Teófilo Cubillas, Alberto Gallardo
Manager: Didi
Scorers: Rivellino (11), Tostão (15, 52), Alberto Gallardo (28), Teófilo Cubillas (70), Jairzinho (75)

Semi-Finals
Uruguay vs Brazil 1-3
17 June 1970, Estadio Jalisco, Guadalajara
Referee: José Maria Ortiz de Mendibil (Spain)
Brazil: Félix; Carlos Alberto, Brito, Wilson Piazza, Everaldo; Clodoaldo, Gérson, Rivellino; Jairzinho, Tostão, Pelé
Manager: Mário Lobo Zagallo

Uruguay: Ladislao Mazurkiewicz, Atilio Ancheta, Roberto Matosas, Luis Ubiña, Juan Mujica, Julio

Castillo, Luis Cubilla, Ildo Maneiro (Víctor Espárrago 74), Julio Cortés, Julio Morales, Dagoberto Fontes
Manager: Juan Hohberg
Scorers: Cubilla (19), Clodoaldo (44), Jairzinho (76), Rivellino (89)

World Cup Final
Brazil vs Italy 4-1
21 June 1970, Estadio Azteca, Mexico City
Referee: Rudi Glöckner (East Germany)
Brazil: Félix; Carlos Alberto, Brito, Wilson Piazza, Everaldo; Clodoaldo, Gérson, Rivellino; Jairzinho, Tostão, Pelé
Manager: Mário Lobo Zagallo

Italy: Enrico Albertosi; Tarcisio Burgnich, Giacinto Facchetti, Pierluigi Cera, Roberto Rosato, Mario Bertini (Antonio Juliano 74), Sandro Mazzola, Giancarlo de Sisti, Gigi Riva, Angelo Domenghini, Roberto Boninsegna (Gianni Rivera 83)
Manager: Ferruccio Valcareggi
Scorers: Pelé (18), Boninsegna (37), Gérson (66), Jairzinho (71), Carlos Alberto (86)

Acknowledgements

BRAZIL IS not a country for beginners, said composer and singer Carlos Tom Jobim. He was right of course – Brazilians can leave one exasperated. But they also enchant as did my unforgettable and incomparable friend, the late Alexandre Gontijo, whose encyclopaedic knowledge of Brazilian football helped me navigate the complexity of Rio de Janeiro.

He helped me with various interviews, including Mário Zagallo and Carlos Alberto Parreira. I thank all the members of the 1970 team who were so generous with their time: Ado, Emerson Leão, José Baldocchi, Brito, Clodoaldo, Carlos Alberto, Dadá Maravilha, Edu, Gérson, Marco Anônio, Paulo Cézar Caju, Rivellino, Rogério Hetmanek, Roberto Miranda, Tostão, Jairzinho, Wilson Piazza and Zé Maria.

I thank Dino Sani and Zito for their recollection of Brazil's first World Cup victory in 1958. Amarildo, Antônio Lima, Rildo and Afonsinho often provided crucial background on Brazilian football in the

1960s, but they were also frank and forthright in their analysis.

Professor Lamartine DaCosta and Raul Milliet, João Saldanha's nephew, shared their wisdom whenever I asked.

I thank Pepe, Patricia Venerando, Paul Van Himst, Silva Batuta, Jair da Costa, Paraná, Manoel Maria, José Augusto, Marcelo Chirol, Abraham Klein, Luís Pereira, Valdomiro, João Vitto Saldanha, Carlos Azevedo, Regis Frati, Luis Taranto, José Fiolo, Wlamir Marques, Orlando Cani and Felipe Muñoz for their stories and insights.

I thank veteran journalists Juca Kfouri, João Maximo and José Trajano for generously enlightening a young journalist.

An avid listener of BBC World Radio in my teens, I'd first written to Tim Vickery in 2001. In those emails I surprisingly never asked him about Brazil's 1970 team. That changed in Rio. Tim became a precious source of unparalleled knowledge, inspiration and encouragement. I dare call him a friend and greatly cherish our coffees at Palacio de Catete.

They made all the sifting through newspaper archives more enjoyable, even if the odour in the reading rooms of Rio's Biblioteca Nacional was sometimes unsettling. The library's online archives, however, are second to none and became an invaluable resource.

I thank Ivan Soter, an encyclopaedia in his own right, for always responding to my countless questions.

I thank Marcelo Neves, Gilmar's son, and colleague Paulo Vitor for generously sharing their address books as I tracked down former players and arranged interviews and I thank André Souza for transcribing many interviews.

Writing a book in a second language is not straightforward. I thank Satish Sekar and Marie Shabaya for their contributions. I am greatly indebted to James Corbett and Jacob Sweetman for their smart editing which greatly improved the book.

I thank Andrew Downie, James Corbett (again), Brian Glanville, Keir Radnedge and Professor Samuel Freedman for their advice and support. They all helped in different but significant ways. At Pitch Publishing, my gratitude goes to Jane Camillin and editor Ivan Butler.

I greet my friends from the early days – Lieven, Marta and Javier – and thank my mum and my brother Sid for sharing my love for the boys from Brazil for so long.

Last but not least, um grande abraço to my Carioca friends – Nelio, Fraga, Nilda, Veloso, Ony, João, Artur, Joost and Henrik. Até breve!

Bibliography

Books

Antônio, M., and Salvador, S., *A Memória da Copa de 70: Equecimentons e Lembranças do Futebol na Construção da Identidade Nacional* (Campinas: Autores Associados, 2009).

Bellos, A., *Futebol. The Brazilian Way of Life* (London: Bloomsbury, 2002).

Caju, P., *Dei a Volta na Vida* (São Paulo: A Girafa, 2006).

Cardoso, T., and Rockmann, R., *O Marechal da Vitória: Uma História de Rádio, TV e Futebol* (São Paulo: A Girafa, 2005).

Castro, R., *Garrincha: The Triumph and Tragedy of Brazil's Forgotten Footballing Hero* (London: Yellow Jersey Press, 2004).

de Almeida, A., and DaCosta L., *Meio Ambiente, Esporte, Lazer e Turismo: Estudos e Pesquisas no Brasil 1967–2007* (Rio de Janeiro: Editora Gama Filho, 2007).

do Nascimiento, E.A., *Pelé. The Autobiography* (London: Simon & Schuster, 2006).

Downie, A., *The Greatest Show on Earth: The Inside Story of the Legendary 1970 World Cup* (Edinburgh: Arena Books, 2021).

Erthal, L., and Borges V., *Zagallo, Um Vencedor* (Rio de Janeiro: ACERJ, 1996).

Garambone, S., *Os 11 Maiores Volantes do Futebol Brasileiro* (São Paulo: Contexto, 2010).

Glanville, B., *The Story of the World Cup* (London: Faber & Faber, 2014).

Goldblatt, D., *The Ball is Round: A Global History of Football* (London: Viking, 2006).

Goldblatt, D., *Futebol Nation: The Story of Brazil Through Soccer* (New York: Nations Books, 2014).

Harris, H., *Pelé: His Life and Times* (London: Robson Books, 2000).

Jenkins, G., *The Beautiful Team: In Search of Pelé and the 1970 Brazilians* (London: Simon & Schuster, 1998).

Macdonald, R., and Batty, E., *Scientific Soccer in the Seventies* (Newton Abbot: Redwood Press, 1972).

McIlvanney, H., and Hopcraft, A., *World Cup '70* (London: Eyre & Spottiswoode, 1970).

Machado, L., *Dadá Maravilha* (Belo Horizonte: Livraria Del Rey, 1999).

Manhães, E., *João Sem Medo – Futebol-Arte e Identidade* (Campinas: Pontes, 2004).

Mario, F., *Viagem em Torno de Pelé* (Rio de Janeiro: Eduator, 1963).

Maximo, J., *João Saldanha* (Rio de Janeiro: Relume-Dumara, 1996).

Milliet, R., *Vida Que Segue: João Saldanha e As Copas de 1966 e 1970* (Rio de Janeiro: Nova Fronteira, 2006).

Muylaert, R., *Barbosa: Um Gol Silencia o Brasil* (São Paulo: Bússola, 2013).

Nogueira, A., *Bola na Rede* (Rio de Janeiro: José Olympio, 1973).

Phillips, N., *Doctor to the World Champions. My Autobiography* (Bloomington: Trafford Publishing, 2009).

Rollin, J., *England's World Cup Triumph* (London, Davies Books, 1966).

Sarmento, C., *A Regra do Jogo: uma História Institucional da CBF* (Rio de Janeiro: CPDOC, 2006).

Siqueira, A., *João Saldanha: Uma Vida em Jogo* (São Paulo: Companhia Editora Nacional, 2007).

Soter, I., *Enciclopédia da Seleção: 100 Anos de Seleção Brasileira de Futebol - 1914 a 2014* (Rio de Janeiro: Folha Seca, 2006).

Soter, I., *Quando a Bola era Rondonda* (Rio de Janeiro: Folha Seca, 2008).

Tostão, *Lembranças, Opinoes, Reflexões sobre Futebol* (São Paulo: Dorea Books and Art, 1997).

Tostão, *A Perfeição Não Existe: Crônicas de futebol* (São Paulo: Três Estrelas, 2011).

Tostão, *Tempos Vividos, Sonhados e Perdidos* (São Paulo: Companhia das Letras, 2016).

Ubberreich, T., *1970: O Brasil é Tri. A Conquista Que Eternizou a Seleção Brasileira* (São Paulo: Letrasdo Pensamento, 2020).

Vilarinho, C., *Quem Derrubou João Saldanha: pe em pratos limpos todos os detalhes de campanha de fritura e demissão do técnico que classificou a seleção Brasileira para a Copa de 1970* (Rio de Janeiro: Livrosdefutebol.com, 2010).

Willemsen, A., *De Goddelijke Kanarie* (Amsterdam: Thomas Rap, 1994).

Willemsen, C., *De Moord op Maradonna* (Amsterdam: De Bezige Bij, 1996).

Wilson, J., *Inverting the Pyramid: A History of Football Tactics* (London: Orion, 2008).

Wilson, J., *The Anatomy of England: A History in Ten Matches* (London: Orion, 2011).

Winner, D., *Brilliant Orange: The Neurotic Genius of Dutch Football* (London: Bloomsbury, 2000).

Zagallo, M., *As Lições da Copa* (Rio de Janeiro: Edições Bloch, 1971).

Journal articles

Cabo, A., and Helal, R., *17 de junho de 1970 – Brasil 3 x1 Uruguai: jornalismo esportivo e acionamento da memória na imprensa uruguaia* (São Paulo: Encontro da Compos, 2008).

Drummond, M., 'Sports and politics in the Brazilian Estado Novo (1937–1945)', *The International Journal of the History of Sport*, 31:10, 1245–1254.

Kasperowksi, D., 'Constructing altitude training standards for the 1968 Mexico Olympics: the impact of ideals of equality and uncertainty', *The International Journal of the History of Sport*, 26:9, 1263–1291, 2009.

Suchý, J. and Waic, M., 'The use of altitude training in sports – from antiquity to present day', *Sport Science*, 10, Suppl 1: 23–33.

Wrynn., A., '"A debt was paid off in tears": science, IOC politics and the debate about high altitude in the 1968 Mexico City Olympics', *The International Journal of the History of Sport*, 23:7, 1152–1172, 2006.

Zolov, E., 'Showcasing the "Land of Tomorrow": Mexico and the 1968 Olympics', *The Americas*, 61: 2 (Oct., 2004), 159–188.

Technical studies

DaCosta, L., *Planejamento Mexico* (Rio de Janeiro: Ministerio da Educação e Cultura, 1967).
FIFA Technical Studies, World Cup 1966, 1970, 1974.
FIFA Technical Study, Olympic Games 1986.

Newspapers and magazines

Correio da Manhã
De Standaard
L'Equipe
Jornal do Brasil
Folha de São Paulo
Handelsblad
Het Volk
Jornal dos Sports
O Cruzeiro
O Globo
The Blizzard
The Daily Mail
The Guardian
The New York Times
The Sunday Times
The Telegraph
Manchete Esportiva
Placar
World Soccer